Tempus ORAL HISTORY Series

Hayling Island
voices

Mesdames Topley, Hughes, Cook and Camp celebrating at St Herman's Caravan Estate in the 1960s.

Tempus ORAL HISTORY *Series*

Hayling Island
voices

Compiled by
Patricia Ross

TEMPUS

First published 2000
Copyright © Patricia Ross, 2000

Tempus Publishing Limited
The Mill, Brimscombe Port,
Stroud, Gloucestershire, GL5 2QG

ISBN 0 7524 2049 6

Typesetting and origination by
Tempus Publishing Limited
Printed in Great Britain by
Midway Clark Printing, Wiltshire

Cover illustration: *Lady Members of Hayling Island Golf Club in the 1920s.*

Noel Pycroft's father and Uncle Bill lacing a net.

Contents

SALTERNS QUAY, HAYLING ISLAND   G.2251

Salterns Quay.

Introduction

We had been living in Hayling for over a year when Dr John Stedman of Portsmouth Museum Service mentioned to us the Portsmouth Oral History Project for the Millennium. I had been researching local history and folklore, with the help of my husband, John, since we retired and it seemed appropriate to turn this interest to our new surroundings. The Wessex Film and Sound Archive was happy to help with advice and pleased to receive tape recordings of the personal stories of Hayling Islanders. So I began my own millennium project: a fascinating, time-consuming and thoroughly enjoyable search for Hayling's twentieth-century past, through the eyes of those who have lived and worked here. They have invited me into their homes and workplaces, served coffee and biscuits and talked about their lives, families, work and leisure. Some have written to tell me of times spent here in war and peace. They were invariably kind and helpful. Their stories weave a picture of joys and sorrows, pride in achievement and incredible personal dedication to community projects. The Hayling Billy railway and the two bridges which have linked the Island to mainland Hampshire loom large in the consciousness of many.

Hayling is the next island eastwards on the coast of Hampshire to the city of Portsmouth. Weak bridges eventually connected it with the mainland in the past and it remained rural long after its hinterland was developed. The population has increased, notably in the 1960s, since the building of the new road bridge. Each further increase in house building has been

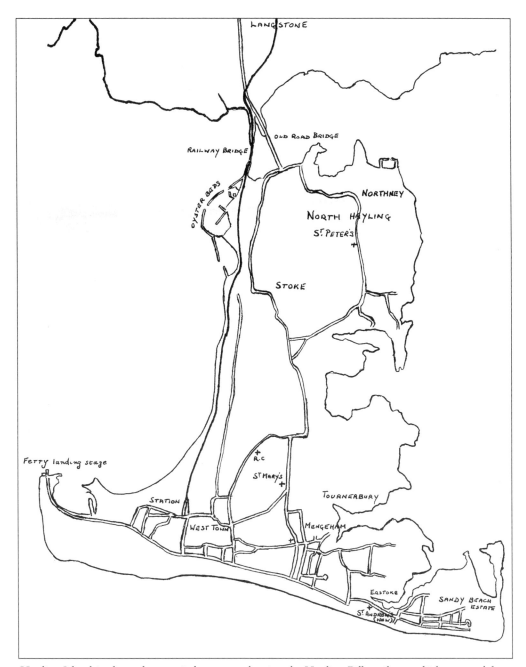

Hayling Island in the early twentieth century showing the Hayling Billy railway which operated from 1867 until 1963.

South Hayling Beach: families enjoying the sea and sand in the 1920s.

vehemently regretted and sometimes hotly opposed by existing residents. However, the Island was described as 'paradise' by a visitor I recently met.

Much of North Hayling is rural still. Those who have lived here all their lives are proud of being Hayling Islanders. Urban South Hayling shares the Island's strong sense of community.

As a newcomer who came to Hayling Island in 1996, I was interested to know where other newcomers had come from and why, as well as to meet established Islanders. Opinions differ as to how long it takes for a newcomer to become an Islander, or whether he or she will ever be 'adopted'. If you stay from two to ten years, it is assumed you will never leave. It is also said, 'If you've ever lived on Hayling, you're sure to return.' Many do.

I chose to interview as wide a variety of people as possible to make recordings and have reluctantly had to leave out, for reasons of time and space, many whom I was told I must talk to. Subjects were suggested to me by members of the Mengham Women's Institute; the Bosmere Hundred Society; Hayling Island Horticultural Society; as well as by friends and neighbours. Three contributors contacted me after my appeal in the *Hayling Islander*. Following responses to a similar appeal in service publications, I have quoted the reminiscences of four former members of the armed services who served here during the Second World War, in addition to those who live on Hayling. Other replies to this appeal have formed the basis of another study. To strike a balance between established and recent residents, I have at times knocked on doors in search of willing volunteers.

Most of the material used is taken from forty-six taped interviews, plus letters in answer to questionnaires sent to people who have moved away. My transcriptions are extracts from subjects' recorded memories, in their own words, with some of the repetition, the 'ands' and 'ers' cut out. I hope this allows for the flavour and feel of the spoken word to come through. Accent is sometimes hinted at by the spelling and punctuation. My own comments are in brackets and included only when they appear to assist clarity.

Some tapes are available, when authorized by the contributors, at the Wessex Film and Sound Archive. Some memories used are from short, face to face conversations which I recorded in note form in as close an approximation to the speakers' own words as I could manage. I recorded a short piece of my own for Chapter 10 as it seemed only fair.

Oral history gives an alternative picture of what matters to ordinary people, which is quite different from the formal history which I learned at school. It is valuable so that future generations may understand our world as we see it. I feel privileged to have shared the memories presented here.

Sadly Mrs Duckett, Mrs Chamberlain and Mr Plimbley have died since they made their recordings. I have included their words, as they wished me to do when the recordings were made. That these stories have survived them demonstrates how important it is to record the past while those who experienced it are still with us.

Patricia Ross
May 2000

The author (left) on a seaside holiday with her brother and a friend in the 1930s.

Foreword

I am delighted to have the opportunity to write a foreword for this marvellous book on Hayling Island, which contains so much oral history. My own memories of the Island, as a native of Hampshire for forty-four years, is of 'sun, sea, fun-fair and ferry'. I first visited in the early 1960s as a child on holiday with my parents, and later revisited with my wife in the 1970s, as well as subsequently. The changes taking place were noticeable, but not so glaring as in other parts of Hampshire, and I was pleased to see that Hayling Island has lost none of its charm for visitors.

My desire to help preserve twentieth-century Hampshire life – and beyond – in audio-visual form stems partly from changes which have taken place in all our lives, especially during the last fifty years or so. Not much film or sound recorded about Hayling Island has reached Wessex Film and Sound Archives, so I am delighted that Pat has been able to record local memories for preservation and access in the form of her oral history tapes. Indeed, her project has also brought copies of videos to the archive, all of which help to inform present and future historians, residents and other interested parties about this corner of Hampshire.

I like oral history as a historical source because it is much more comprehensive than writing notes, more spontaneous and less selective, knows no social or gender boundaries, and is full of detail which could be invaluable in the future. Modern sound recording equipment is very portable and good enough in quality, when used properly, to provide a valuable contribution to local history through recorded memories. This includes accent and, if you are lucky, dialect. Contrary to popular belief, living memories do not necessarily dim with age and can help bring history alive, whilst reminding older folk of their shared experiences. Pat has achieved this with her project and shown that living memories are as valid as any other source of history. I congratulate her on bringing the voices of ordinary people to your attention in this book, and for showing the other side of the coin to official records and history books.

David M. Lee
Film and Sound Archivist
Hampshire Record Office
Winchester

CHAPTER 1

General Memories of the Island

Children gathering to watch a Punch and Judy show on Hayling Beach in the 1930s.

Gone Fishing

Thirty years ago we caught whiting.
I know, old man, in your prime
the great sea bass
thrashed on your line.
Your grandson followed the wavering lamp
of your Hercules bicycle
to the shore for the midnight tide
where we cast, standing in the surf.
Lines baited for those long-gone bass,
We'd catch whiting.
It was a sad story even then,
but not without its moments.
Of secret cigarettes
and hot tea from the Thermos
as the glowing hands of your
service-issue watch
crept up upon 2 a.m.
But sadder still, casting here alone
awash in white spume
and gravel spin
I catch nothing at all,
And have given up smoking.

Nigel Ford

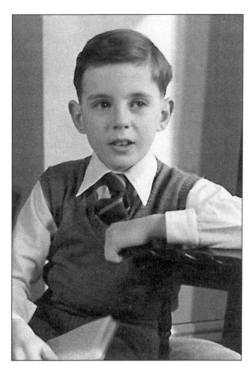

Nigel Ford used to fish off Hayling Beach with his grandfather, H.R. Jackson.

Building the Nab Club

My father had the Nab Club built. It opened 1 April 1935; he also built the guest-house now known as the Kittiwake. We had one girl to help in the shop with Miss Tickner, and Dot Scarterfield, whose brother had the butcher's shop near the Rose in June, was behind the bar. The Regal picture-house was opened by Gracie Fields.

Mrs Mary Voller (née Tickner), born 1923

Ladybirds on the Beach

The year we had the ladybirds – they came from France – there was loads and they were biting, too. They were everywhere. We went down to the beach, they were all on the water. I don't know what's happened to the sea, you don't see a crab in there; always used to.

Mrs Lilian Townsend-Holmes, born 1930

Doorstep Deliveries

Even after the war, coal was delivered, groceries, everything. People used to come round with horse and carts and little delivery vans; milk was delivered with a float, from Walters' Dairy, just by Ham Field. They had a dairy shop. The pub on the corner – the Barley Mow – was part of the farm; the Barley Mow was where the bakers [Heidi's] is now.

Woodward's got bombed and moved to near the station, and moved back. There were about three families lived here [on the Warren Sands Estate] during the war and a bookbinder to the royal family. Noel Pycroft made them a wheelbarrow – he wheeled it all the way from North Hayling. The rest was taken over by the military.

Mrs A., born 1920

Remembering the Abdication

There were houses on one side of Staunton Avenue and cows in fields that used to look at you over the fence as you went down to the beach. The abdication of Edward VIII: I remember sitting on the sea-shore down by Langstone Harbour with a boy-friend and thinking, 'Oh, dear!' – you know? – 'My goodness me, how exciting!' So I remember that, of course.

Mrs Brenda Wood, born 1915

The Road to Sandy Point

You knew everybody. In fact, the old locals wouldn't go down past Eastoke Corner towards Sandy Point because that was 'a den of sin'. There was supposed to have been a house of ill repute. And people swam in the nude. Things like that! Course we went down, as kids.

Peter Tibble, born 1932

Haircut and Rag-Worms!

Some of my older customers have told me that next to my shop [Barrett's Shoe Repairs, Elm Grove] there was a barber's with a proper barber's pole [now Home Sweet Home]. Cliff was the proprietor. It was like a club, people used to sit around and chat about the war. It was also a fishing-tackle shop. Someone would be having his hair cut and a customer would come in asking for half a pound of rag-worms, and the barber would reach over and weigh out the rag-worms and go right back to cutting hair.

Clive Barrett, born 1956

The Freeze of 1940

1940 was a very harsh winter, it was common practice for pipes to freeze, not everyone had permanent heating.

A.A.F. Bell, born 1927

Home and Hairdressing

The hairdresser, Ellen Bursby, went round on a bicycle. She had a house, and a salon

Bungalow Town, Eastoke Corner.

Staunton Avenue and Station Road, South Hayling.

was built on the front. Mr Tibble senior had a stall next to it.

Mrs Mary Voller (née Tickner), born 1923

New Home at North Hayling

I got to North Hayling. All the houses were Pycroft home-built bricks; when we wanted a repair, we went to Mr Pycroft for the same bricks again. And Wilf Penny, he saw to any building things.

I waited on the house to be built and my daughter's birthday was 23 September. We moved in at the end of September and at the beginning of October we had the tide five stairs up, flooding. The bathroom was downstairs. On the Saturday we put the big gallon can of varnish behind the bath, and there's the tide flooding up and up and my daughter said, 'Mummy, quick! Come and look at all the pretty colours coming out of the bathroom!' And for years all – so high, round the wall – the chairs, table legs, was all varnish. We were a good couple of fields away from the water, but the bank had burst. And I watched it come flooding over. And the electric meters and things went off with a bang under the stairs, and that was in October, about 1944? Must have been.

Mrs Queenie Gates, born 1903

Dentures Overboard!

My father worked on a car park and on the construction of the New Bridge – during which he fell out of a boat and lost his dentures. They were found three days later, washed up by the tide. It was very fortunate.

Mrs Audrey Cozens (née Tyrrell), born 1939

CHAPTER 2

Parents, Grandparents and Families

The ferry arriving at Hayling Island. The notice reads 'Please do not deposit sand in ferry boats'.

The Ferry Boat Inn

The Hayling ferry itself was run by my grandmother's relations. My grandmother, who died in 1986, in her ninety-ninth year, was Alice Derben; she was born at Dean Lane End. Her mother died in childbirth when she was a little girl; she was brought up by her aunt at the Ferry Boat Inn. The Spraggs – they were the landlords – were related to her. There are still Spraggs about. They ran the ferry and the Ferry Boat Inn. One of my grandmother's relatives said that Martha Spraggs was a very kind and loving person and my grandmother was one of the family. He said then, the harbour was black with sail of an evening, as the big ships came in to shelter for the night and the captains would be rowed to the Ferry Boat Inn for Martha Spraggs' cooking. My grandmother was born in 1887 and she went there when she was thirteen or fourteen. She subsequently met and married my grandfather, who helped to lay the golf course. He was John Derben.

Mrs Janet Bocking, born 1939

John Derben (1880-1942), his wife Alice (née Bastable) and their son Alfred John, known as Jack.

The Yacht Haven

My father worked at Yacht Haven, Copse Lane, which he helped to build. It was mainly a repair yard for big yachts; the skippers used to come and live with us. The yacht harbour silted up and Yacht Haven eventually burned down.

David Roberts, born 1933

Honeymoon on Bright's Lane

My grandfather and family bought this land right at the beginning of 1900 and my father was not allowed to be in the First World War because they found he had a heart murmur. His father had bought this house about 1912. And my mother and father were married in 1913 and they came down for their honeymoon into it and then my father's health improved. They bought the rest of the land – in those days our land was all of the south side of Bright's Lane.

Mrs Brenda Wood, born 1915

Summer in Boat and Bungalow

My grandparents bought a boat which they had before the Great War. They had it down at Mengham with my parents, teenagers then. Ultimately they brought what was a big, old sailing-boat, dismantled, down to Langstone Harbour, right up the creek, and there were no other boats there. When they got married, and my first cousin was born, my grandfather thought it was too dangerous out there so he had this boat brought in onto the shore in the Kench, round in the private part, where the bungalows are now. My grandfather built a bungalow, and later on my father built a bungalow, so we've always spent our summers there. My grandfather lived in Southsea and latterly we lived at Farlington.

Mrs Hazel Warner, born 1929

Hayling Becomes Home

I got two sisters. My eldest sister lives down on the Seafront. My dad came to Hayling as a bricklayer. I've lived here all my life.

Lawrence Shepherd, born 1927

L. Shepherd's youngest sister, Jean Bright, as Boots in a Northney Village Hall pantomime.

Grace Townsend's great-great-grandfather who was a shepherd at Stairs Farm.

Grandfather at Stairs Farm

There was an old farm opposite the council houses in 1926 which used to belong to my grandfather. Grandfather had animals, sheep and things, 'cos he was a shepherd, my grandfather and my old great-uncle, yes. The Landsleys and I can go back about four or five generations in the church there [St Mary's]. There was the Landsleys and the Dollerys, there's quite a lot, we were all sort of cousins.

Mrs Grace Townsend, born 1924

Sandy Point Road

My father and mother, Mr and Mrs R. Tickner, had bought the farm down Sandy Point Road, Hayling, in 1916. My sister and two brothers were born in the farmhouse, and I was born there on 15 July 1923. My father owned 136 acres of which only the Creek Road bit was flooded.

Mrs Mary Voller (née Tickner), born 1923

Gasworks Baby

Dad, he was a carpenter. O' course, my grandfather was manager of the old Hayling gasworks on the island in the late 1800s. My father was born round by the gasworks.

Colin Vaughn, born 1932

Harry Landsley celebrated his ninetieth birthday at the West Town Hotel, c. 1960.

Hayling Coal and Transport's horse and cart making deliveries near the West Town Hotel, now the West Town public house, on Station Road.

Running the West Town Hotel

My father and grandparents came from London, during the First World War. Hayling was very rural. My grandfather took the West Town Hotel, and my father's first impressions were, 'Oh, what a horrible place!' There was no street lighting, and it was raining – he got used to it!

Shortly after he came here, Grandfather was called away to the war and my father was left with my grandmother to run the West Town Hotel. To try and make ends meet, they had a taxi at the hotel and he took to driving it, at only fourteen! I don't think they had licences in those days. It was local trade, there were lots of really large houses and

quite well-known people, and the West Town Hotel used to service the parties they used to have with food and drink. The selling of the big houses mainly happened during the Second World War and afterwards, and then the estates got broken up and housing estates were built on the sites.

Michael Camp, born 1933

Head Gardener to Nurseryman

I was born in Hayling, in Stamford Avenue. My father was head gardener for the McEuens at Richmond House. We lived in the gardener's cottage on the estate. Father

THE WEST TOWN

ALEHOUSE

An evocative modern pub sign, Station Road.

knew every one of his workers, Christian and surname; he never passed you without saying, 'Good morning' and these other people o'course, they were different. They sort of couldn't care a tinker's cuss, basically, so my father thought, right! He'd get out. So my father bought the shop and nursery in Elm Grove.

The original shop was at Nos 44 and 46. The house still stands, the driveway is an entrance to the Health Centre. The Health Centre stands on the site of the nursery. We sold it to the Health Centre. Father bought the nursery in 1936.

He'd served in the artillery during World War One. Because he worked in agriculture he was not directed into other employment in 1939; he was a first-aider. I think Pop was about eighteen or nineteen when the First World War started, so he went through the whole war.

Peter Tibble, born 1932

had been inside-fruit foreman to Sir John Shelley-Rolls at Avington Park. Lady Rolls was a descendant of the poet and he, o'course, was one of the Rolls-Royce Rolls.

I think Mr McEuen's father had made his money out of copra – there's a plaque in St Mary's. The McEuens had cooks and maids and several gardeners. Father came here as head gardener. He had several men under him. The estate in Stamford Avenue was bounded by Bacon Lane, Staunton Avenue and the Seafront. There was a house built on the far south-west corner.

Mr Gilbert bought out the McEuens, and he bought lots of land around the Island. My father wasn't too keen on the Gilberts, because they weren't quite the sort of gentry that he'd been used to. They were one of the *nouveaux riches*, they didn't have the breeding and the way to treat people, in contrast to Sir John Shelley-Rolls, who

Pycroft Family Brick-Makers

My grandfather, William Henry, came here in 1901 from Portsmouth. He made bricks in Portsmouth; his mother's family made bricks in Portsmouth, had been making bricks for 200 years.

The brickyards were very simple. There was a field here this year and a brickyard next year but it was all they had, the earth. They dug the earth into ridges, to dry a bit, then made the bricks; it was just all hand-worked. They had a slip mould.

Mother was a Miss Powell. Algernon Powell had the milk round, mother's father. Powells come to Hayling in 1856 from Forest Side, took Northney Farm. The doctor said to my Powell grandmother that she would fill the house with babies and die, which is what she done. She had seventeen children in twenty-four years. Father was a brick-maker. He also worked on the farm at home and went fishing, shooting and duck shelling [punt gunning for ducks]. Father had to stop brick-making, they weren't allowed to burn the bricks during the First World War. He was in the Volunteers at sixteen and a half. Volunteers from Hayling went to Fort Nelson by bicycle for rifle training.

Noel Pycroft, born 1928

A Bungalow in Two Weeks

My father built the bungalow: he bought this plot of land down Westhaye Road, 40 bob a foot, but he had to build within three months. 'Cos, they wanted him to have the whole of Eastoke to develop, but he was too busy in London, so he just bought one plot. An' then he brought down several workmen – I think there were about eight of them – and they stayed along at the Coast Guard Cottages for a couple of weeks and built the bungalow! In a couple of weeks! They used to go home at the weekend. We came to live here in 1946, with Mum and Dad.

Mrs Mavis Chamberlain (née Tucker), 1936-2000

Swimming and Sand-Yachting

My father was wonderful, he'd swim with us and he bought us an old raft so that we could learn to swim out, and anchored the raft off, so we learned all the difficulties of the water. And my first introduction to sailing was in a

A Congregational church sale of work. Mavis Chamberlain's mother, Mrs Tucker, is third from the left.

Alfred Thomas Derben (1846-1937), the third generation of Tournebury brickmakers, was Janet Bocking's great-grandfather and the father of John Derben (1880-1942).

sand-yacht which my father built. You go by the wind; oh yes, sand-yachting feels exactly the same as sailing on water.

In the 1939 war, he was requisitioning officer for Winchester; he was an estate agent and surveyor.

Beryl, Lady Mackworth, born 1915

A Derben Family Tree

My great-great-great-grandfather, John Derben [born about 1774] was a brick-maker on Hayling in the early 1800s at the Tournebury brickyard. And the two brothers – that was my great-grandfather, and his brother – built the house called Glenleigh in Church Road [later named Musketeers]. The one family lived in half and the brother with his wife and daughter lived in the other half. That was built with Derben bricks. All along the South Coast, they were used. They traded with salt and bricks, I suppose by boat if the bricks went off the Island. I suppose the Old Bridge was built, once they were making a lot [the Old Bridge was built in 1823]. The salt would go off and then something else would come back. They walked everywhere, they used to go to the Sunday school and I've got their little prizes, Walter and John.

When the brick works folded, my grandfather of course did the greenkeeping

Alice Derben (née Bastable) retired from the postal service in 1919.

Hayling sports, 1913. The little boy (front left) is Janet Bocking's father, Alfred John Derben.

[at Hayling golf course] and his brother Walter helped him with that.

My grandfather, John Derben, had rheumatic fever when he was thirty. His was manual work, as a greenkeeper. He was left crippled, they nursed it with absolute bed-rest. And when he got out of bed he couldn't walk. And they paid someone in London to sort of straighten out his feet and he was able to walk. He always had very bad legs.

My uncle George Derben, because he wasn't safe on his stick outside and because there was no frame as such in those days, he used a chair as a frame. He was crippled with arthritis, he could hardly move with it. The only time I can ever remember him coming out was every Christmas Day. My Aunt Bess used to arrive about half an hour before him. He died in his eighties. His childhood was at the brickyard until it closed down. Then afterwards they lived in Glenlea, Church Road. He was the eldest so he was born

'Big Aunt Bess', Elizabeth Emma Derben, with her brother George Derben.

The Derben family's Tournebury brickyard.

about 1870-1875. When they worked as hard as they did, they used to age.

My father, of course, was brought up at Sinah Farm and then at the golf-club. And Grandmother lived there until she came to live at Pandora, which was the house her husband and she had had built in Church Road, and it's still there. Grandfather never lived in it and grandmother had rented it out.

Mrs Janet Bocking, born 1939

Oyster-beds in the Mill-Pond

We moved to Portsmouth when I was about four years old, but at the outbreak of the first war, my dad was called up – he was a reservist – and we moved back to Emsworth to my grandparents. I would be about ten. Well, my grandparents were fishermen, with boats going out and coming in, when they could get out, when there was no restrictions in the harbour.

We lived next to the old mill, that was our playroom, in the mill house. It was a flour mill, and a water-mill. It had a big wheel. You must have seen the mill-pond? Well, we lived next to the mill. My grandfather, he had oyster-beds in the mill-pond. The mill was owned by Dittman & Malpas; they had big pleasure yachts, and my grandad used to what he called 'vittal' them. If they were going out sailing, he would make sure that the crew was there and that they had whatever they wanted.

Mrs Queenie Gates, born 1903

The Electrical Engineer's Son

My father was a Portsmouth electrical engineer who held amateur radio licence No. 1. So I was brought up with winding coils and transformers.

F.T. Skipper, born 1932

CHAPTER 3

Childhood

Mavis Chamberlain and her friend Pauline Berry at Eastoke Beach.

Memories of Summertime

When I was a teenager, Valerie Pycroft and and I used to go to a girls' club at St Mary's church and Noel used to come and meet Valerie, when we were about fifteen, you know. I used to belong to the bike club at St Mary's too. We had a badge embroidered with a bicycle wheel. We used to go off cycling at the weekend and that. When I was three or four I came to Hayling, my father built a bungalow down Westhaye Road. We

used to come down for the whole of the summer. I lost my friend, and this photograph is of her and me when we were children.

Mrs Mavis Chamberlain (née Tucker),
1936-2000

Fishing in the Harbour

All I remember as a child is masses of green fields, lots of birds, lots of flowers, lots of blackberries. I lived off Rails Lane, by the big garage. As a boy, I used to be an angler. In a couple of hours you could always reckon to catch two or three or a dozen nice plaice, easily. My grandfather had an old boat. I used to row it off down the harbour to fish.

Roy Smith, born 1923

A Play-Pen on the Beach

When the children were little, I used to take the play-pen to the beach, because it had a floor in it, it was literally across the road from our flat. I had them all one straight after the other, that's why I had the twin push-chair. I used the Mengham village shops, the library, and obviously the children went to school on Hayling. Then they went on to South Downs College, all three of them. By bus. I mean, they managed fine. I couldn't drive anyhow.

When they first started school I used to walk them there but they preferred to come home on the school bus. It dropped them up in Southwood Road, just at the top, because the Warren Sands Estate has two entrances, there's the white gate and you had a key and you'd just walk up the road and meet them through that, near St Andrew's church. Well, I was at the corner of Bembridge and Clover Drive. We just used to go across to the beach from the top flat, you see. I remember following my son round the corner to Riley's newsagents, he was not four, he didn't know I was following him, but they were safer then. They could go to school and come home alone at quite a young age. In fact Hayling

Pat Gordon's children, Bruce and Kay, on the merry-go-round at the fun-fair.

The Hayling ferry.

was probably a lot safer for a lot longer than the big places, don't you think?

Mrs Patricia Gordon, born 1943

Born Before Boundary Changes

My mother had gone to see her mother and father in Bournemouth and I was born either on the station, on the train or on the bus to the hospital – one or the other. An' I never forgave her 'cos o'course, it's Dorset now, not Hampshire, isn't it?! But my parents lived in Church Road, Hayling.

My dad came back safe from the war. I don't know how he came back safe. I think he went over just after the invasion – but he was in the Royal Engineers – so he was involved in all the preparation of laying roads, all that sort of thing.

John Derben OBE, born 1937

Holidays from Southsea

As a small child, we came over as holiday people; my father had to go back to Southsea and work. Even when I was five years old, we came across with Nanny and the big pram, with everything – walked, right from Devonshire Avenue in Southsea – walked, me, at five years old! Came across the ferry. The ferry-boat had to go round in a circle to get to the other pontoon. I used to put my ear against it to listen to it buzzing.

Mrs Brenda Wood, born 1915

After School in Summer

The children used to come home from school and in summer I'd make sandwiches and we'd walk down to the beach and have lunch. It was beautiful.

Mrs Beryl Bonniface

L. Shepherd's youngest sister and two of his daughters, with Johnny Peel at Northney Village Hall.

The Hayling Majorettes

Both the girls belonged to the Hayling Majorettes, in fact they were founder-members. Mrs Kelly used to run the Majorettes. I can't remember when they folded. My middle daughter was still helping with them in her twenties, then of course she moved away and got married. My son had a paper round and he used to go and sweep the greens before they started golf, at one time. I wasn't able, when I was young, to have a little job. It wasn't done. And my mother was an invalid. So my children had more freedom than I did. But they always

had little pocket-money jobs. When my son was at college, he used to go and help out at the New Town Hotel.

Mrs Patricia Gordon, born 1943

Home-Made Radios

I was born in Eastney at Portsmouth in January of 1932 and I stayed there until the bombs got really bad about 1942. At nine, I was building rectifiers and TRF radios and all that. We used to make our own. Father made his own loudspeakers.

F.T. Skipper, born 1932

Lawrence Shepherd as a boy riding on the greengrocer's pony at Northney.

Henry Durrel with the Union flag, behind Troop Leader Colin Vaughn, at a St Mary's church parade. Lined up behind the Scouts are Guides and Sea Rangers, from left to right: ? Cleeve, ? Muxworthy, Christine Cannings, ? Spooner, Wendy Hurford, and Elizabeth Taylor.

Free to Play

I was born in Manor Road council houses, opposite Higworth. As children, we enjoyed ourselves. We had to make our own entertainment really, mainly Scouting, football and just playing in general, over on the shores and in the copses.

Colin Vaughn, born 1932

Busy Days

I spent most of my school holidays with my Nana in Newcastle. The pace of life was so much different, wasn't it? It just seemed to be filled up with going to school and finding your own entertainments. I used to read books and we certainly didn't have television. The first time we had television was for the Queen's Coronation and thereafter our programmes were chosen for us. The TV was in the lounge and we didn't go in the lounge very often. My father had a study and then the dining-room was where we spent a lot of our time. There was always a nice fire in there.

I was in the Guides. Of course Sundays were always taken up with church, three times a day, I had to go. It was Mass, Sunday school and benediction. It was Catholic. I went to a convent day-school, then to a convent boarding-school.

Mrs Patricia Gordon, born 1943

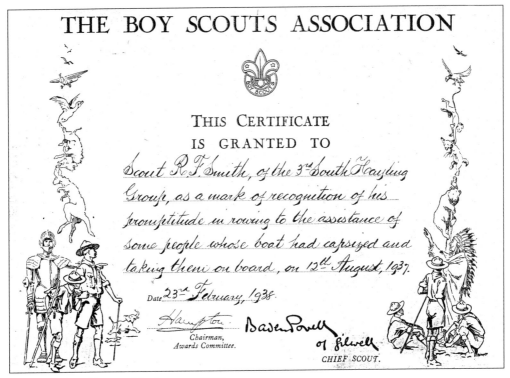

THE BOY SCOUTS ASSOCIATION

THIS CERTIFICATE
IS GRANTED TO

Scout R.F. Smith, of the 3rd South Hayling Group, as a mark of recognition of his promptitude in rowing to the assistance of some people whose boat had capsized and taking them on board, on 12th August, 1937.

Date *23rd February, 1938.*

Hampton
Chairman,
Awards Committee.

Baden Powell of Gilwell
CHIEF SCOUT.

Scout R.F. Smith's award for bravery, 1938.

Castaways on the Sandbank

We used to row to the sandbank, nobody else had ever been there, it was like *Robinson Crusoe*. We had a wonderful life.

Mrs Hazel Warner, born 1929

Halçyon Days at Hayling

I was born in Drayton, greater Portsmouth, the fourth child of five. The family came to Hayling because, after the Second World War, my father realized he really couldn't keep two houses going. We moved into our Hayling cottage in 1919.

Hayling was very different in those days; the roads were all sand, and after the First World War we saved by never having any shoes, the whole of the summer we walked about in bare feet. There was nobody on the beach at all. There was one family from, I think, Hungerford – you got to know – right through the early 1920s. Of course we were driven together, but they were halçyon days, no worries at all. Our house was at Eastoke Corner, a little house called Orme Cottage, where Riley's the bookshop is now.

Beryl, Lady Mackworth, born 1915

Going to the Pictures

There was the cinema, the Regal; we used to go about three nights a week. Sometimes we'd go to Havant, to the pictures. That made four times. We didn't get fed up. We had clubs, played table tennis – I belonged to the church club, was a Boy Scout, there was loads to do. At home we had a little billiard-table, I had my air guns. Most times I used to shoot to protect the crops. There was loads of pigeons about. Fishing, we used to go down to the beach. As a child, you didn't cast out very far, with a handline, but you'd always come home with two or three flounders, sometimes four.

Peter Tibble, born 1932

Oyster Fishermen

I was five years old. We came and lived in the brickyard in the summer. We had oyster-beds at the bottom of the garden. The men that worked on the oyster-beds worked on yachts and they raced in America. They rode their bicycles to my mother's house and then walked down the garden to the oyster-beds. They were oyster fishermen, you see; they worked for J.D. Foster in the winter and in the summer they went yachting.

Noel Pycroft, born 1928

Grandfather's Garden

We used to come and stay in the chalets for all the holidays: Whitsun and summer, and sometimes Easter if it was warm enough. Although there was a house there, my grandmother was a town lady, she wouldn't come, so she stayed in Southsea. Grandfather came over every Monday with his bicycle and his panniers on each side, with all the food for the week, and stayed in his chalets and went back on Friday or Saturday because, of course, they were

Basil, Noel and Derek Pycroft with their father and mother at the brickyard in the 1930s.

religious people so they had to be seen at church together. There are still people here now who remember that his land went through from West Town to Manor Road, and there was a little white gate. When we got to that gate, we used to say, 'We're in Hayling!' Through it he had the most fantastic garden. He had a little garden chair with a big bell. People used to go in, ring the bell, 'Mr Jackson?' they would say, 'Could we have some flowers?' And for one shilling he would pick them a large bunch.

Mrs Brenda Wood, born 1915

A Happy Childhood

I was born in a flat above the old post office on the Seafront. We moved to the council houses in Elm Grove in 1926, to No. 10. It was lovely living here. It was very rural.

During the summers, with my brother – he was younger than me – we used the beach a lot. He died in Austria and he was a lovely fellow. We used to go down to the beach down Seagrove Avenue, it was just a rough track in those days, from our house in the council estate. We'd take a packed lunch, we were so happy. Mum, she used to have to come and drag us home.

We had the Band of Hope, we went out to Bognor, Chichester, Winchester. We never went very far because they were low charabancs in those days.

Mrs Grace Townsend, born 1924

The Secret Garden

There was this lovely walled garden, I called it 'the secret garden'; nobody used it, you could creep away in these places. I was four. With peaches and that round, and o'course

This treasured postcard shows children building sand-castles on Hayling Beach.

The 'Little White Ribbons', a chapel group pictured here in the early twentieth century.

apple trees. The plots were all shaded by box hedging and I can smell box hedge anywhere. It's a wonderful smell.

Peter Tibble, born 1932

Helping on the Farm

We had such a happy time as children, walking to school through the fields and lanes. We all had to help on the farm every Saturday. I had to clean the chicken house out and most evenings my sister and I had to clean the dairy; also we all helped plant potatoes. My father would go up the field with the horses and plough and we came behind, planting. Mother would pluck and dress the chickens and make butter.

One day, my father was chased by our bull, but got out of the field thanks to the cowman. My brother was buried in the sand while playing on the beach; it was touch and go for a few hours but he made it. One Sunday, we were all dressed in our best to go to Sunday school when my sister fell in the sheep-dip; apart from a fright, she was not hurt.

There were very few houses down Sandy Point Road then. In one lived Mr Cole and his wife. He looked after the hospital gardens. We children used to play with the five Cole sons. We all played on the beach and swam in the sea most days in summer, or went winkling.

Mrs Mary Voller (née Tickner), born 1923

Hard Work for the Family

Of course, my mother had a lot of children (nine) so some of us had to get out to make room for the new ones, you see. My brother

Fishing on South Hayling Beach. Mackerel boats went out to a shoal, ran a net around it and pulled the fish on to shore where customers waited on the beach.

joined the Army and I worked in a Portsmouth office but had to go into service from seventeen. It was, I suppose, the thing in those days for us poor people. My dad was a dockyard labourer in Portsmouth. It was hard going for my poor mother but she was a lovely mother. She made and mended, sometimes worked, and we always came first.

Mrs Eva Prior, born 1910

From the Bath House to the Sea

The beach had more sand than now. We could ride our ponies along it, not even waiting for low tide, and there was the old Bath House, a big, wooden shelter with seats in the sides and no roof. It was free. You went in there and changed into your bathing things. There was coir matting

down over the pebbles to the water. I remember walking towards the sea with my mother, and a gentleman, who was lounging on the beach, said, 'Mmm, good pair of legs, and she ain't no chicken!' Mother just sort of tossed her head and walked on, you know? She was one of those kind of people!

Mrs Brenda Wood, born 1915

Cockling and Shrimping

We went on the water – our first trip down the harbour was Whit Monday, always. We often went out, I hated it. Hate the water even now. And we'd go cockling. In sand. My grandfather sold the cockles, 'cos that was his trade. I had a cousin and three sisters, and that was the boatload. And I used to go and help him shrimping. Take the shrimp nets out.

That was on the water, with the trawl-net for the trawling, and no, I didn't like that either. I had to do it. He'd say, 'Come on, we're going shrimping' and Whit Monday was always the trip, weather permitting. We used to pack the basket with sandwiches and off we'd go.

Mrs Queenie Gates, born 1903

Fishing From the Beach

I was the first one to start fishing in my family. From childhood, fishing from the beach then selling what we caught, round the roads, from a bucket, mainly bass. When we were kids, in the shallows you could see big shoals of them. We used to chase them. You could never catch the things but we tried hard to. We progressed to night fishing down the beach. Twenty or thirty bass was easy in a night then, but you don't even see them these days.

When we were kids we used to hang around the Hayling pontoon and get free trips out with the charter boats. You made the tea, but you could still fish. Then you went out with the commercial fishermen. You pick things up from other people, really.

Ian Griffiths, born 1964

Little Islanders

When I came to the Island, my daughter Carol was three months old, her brother about eighteen months. They've been here all their lives, they're Hayling Islanders now; and my young son was born here in 1941, in a basement flat at the Crescent, so he's a Hayling Islander.

Mrs Lilian Townsend-Holmes, born 1930

Christopher Pycroft and Mandy Brown, c. 1962. Christopher holds up a 10lb bass for the camera.

Coronation sports at Northney, 1953. Alan Nichol is second from the left in the front row.

Running to Watch the Lifeboat

When we were children, living in Orme Cottage, if we were not at school when the maroon went off, we'd run along to the old lifeboat station, watch the lifeboat being launched. And o'course, I remember seeing it rowing out through the great breakers and setting their sails.

And I can remember seeing yachts in trouble, in the breakers out here, and being very perturbed about it. When they brought the lifeboat in, we children were always hanging around, they'd give us a ride, and it was pulled up by the horses into the shed. So I've kept in touch with the lifeboat ever since.

Beryl, Lady Mackworth, born 1915

Woollen Swimming-Costumes

I think my mother in those days bought a job lot of wool, it was a burnt orange colour and she knitted me swimming-costumes and a sun-dress; but she used to make me wear my vest under my sun-dress to keep me warm! The bathing-costume, when wet, it used to get sand all in it and drag down to the ground.

Mrs Mavis Chamberlain (née Tucker),
1936-2000

Teenage Years Together

In their teenage years, in a group, my children would go sailing, cycle, take

On this page: *launching the Hayling lifeboat in the early years of the twentieth century. The spectators are watching so calmly, this must have been an exercise!*

picnics, play tennis in friends' gardens.

We had a tennis-court here but it had fallen into disrepair and now there are lots of houses built on it. They played cricket, they would play board games in the house, and at weekends, quite often their friends – who were boarders at Churcher's College – would come down. They would sing and play the piano and just generally get together.

My daughter was a member of the Young Communicants at St Mary's and their scooter club in the 1950s. There was very much going to friends' houses, then. That was just fun, to have a party, but always they tidied up after them and that was fine. You knew exactly where they were. If they were going to be a bit late then they would ring.

There was a cinema, the Regal; a group of them would go there. We knew who they were

Mr L. Shepherd takes a break from cartering to give a local child a ride on the horse.

with, and there was a comfortable set of rules which were not prohibiting but it was just a question of good manners.

Mrs A., born 1920

The West End in the 1920s

At the West end of Hayling now there are houses on the Kench side. In those days there were only old houseboats. The St Mary's Road cinema [now St Mary's Road postal sorting office] had a corrugated-iron roof; black and white films. When we had a thunderstorm or heavy rain, you couldn't hear a thing! I remember going to a film with Dempster the boxer in it. My cousin was so excited he hit me on the nose and I arrived home in floods of blood! I think it was 9d to go in.

Mrs Brenda Wood, born 1915

Family Holidays and Freedom

I moved here with my parents when I was seventeen so really that was their decision; we came down here on holiday when I was about six years old. My dad being in business, my parents bought a place down here so we could come for weekends. Then I used to spend my holidays here, eleven weeks in the summer, very often not just with my mother, my grandparents would come for a while and our dog. It was a safe place. When I was about ten I used to disappear with friends down to the creek, crabbing, boating and so on, come back when we were hungry, late at night. Nobody worried. Mother used to know more or less where I was. It was a great place to be free in.

Eric Dossetter, born 1942

CHAPTER 4

Schools and Hospitals

VAD (Voluntary Aid Detachment) nurses and patients outside the Cresent, where there was a hospital
during the First World War.

School Remains the Same

When we went to school there was only
about 300 children; there was only one
council school, and it was the same when
my daughter, now fifty, went there. But she
was able to go to Warblington [mainland
secondary] at thirteen.

Mrs Grace Townsend, born 1924

On to Havant High School

We went to various schools on the Island,
private schools, and then we went to
Havant, and Havant High School, which
was run by a marvellous man. We used to
have one whole day speaking in French,
which was wonderful.

Beryl, Lady Mackworth, born 1915

Playing Together

I used to take my children to open days at the school at Sandy Point [Lord Mayor Treloar]. It had some very poorly people in. I mean, they were really disfigured. But my children never noticed that, they were all playing ring-a-ring-a-roses with them, they were enjoying themselves.

Mrs Lilian Townsend-Holmes, born 1930

University out of Reach

My parents couldn't afford to send me to university; only rich people went in those days.

F.T. Skipper, born 1932

Teaching

In 1935 I came to teach in Hayling. That school was just the little brick building that you see now, the front bit, the land was all the same; and then there was just one annex that went down, that also was the brick part, and that was all. And every class had forty-eight children.

There was a lot of outside activity. We didn't have a hall, and because it was country you could get out and do things outside, so I don't think you felt quite as restricted as you might have done. But the thing was, it was a very mixed group of children and the next lady to me, who had the seven-year-olds – no one ever came out of that class who couldn't read, not one! And when you think that there were gipsies in it, and a child who was almost deaf and dumb – you know, there were no special schools.

You taught the alphabet but you taught the phonic method as well. You always taught the multiplication tables, and you did a lot of mental arithmetic – nobody had computers!

Hayling School in the 1930s had lino and these horrible desks that tip up and make an awful noise when you stand up, with great, big, iron bits on the end. It was changed when I was there to desks with all those horrible ink-wells, but there were chairs by the desks. So, when we got the chairs, that was a wonderful resolution, because we could just move them all round the classroom. And most of us who were, you know, quite modern because we had just been newly trained, we did do that.

It was a junior school, it went up to eleven – it was in the days of the eleven-plus. And there was a lot of physical training, a lot of football, which was all voluntary, and I used to think to myself, even then, it was terrible because you weren't insured, and the teachers were all doing that on a voluntary basis.

Mrs Brenda Wood, born 1915

To School by Bus

At first they went to a nursery school in Park Road; they had to walk quite a way, or they would go on a fairy-cycle or tricycle. One knew they were safe.

Their next school was at the Pound. That was all ages then, infants to seniors. My daughter didn't go to the local school but to Havant, by bus. Oh, one didn't have a car to fetch and carry. Children got used to going on buses on their own.

Mrs A., born 1920

Dancing Lessons

I had my parents on the Island, who were wonderful. And at that time I was starting the dancing school. I did teach first in the village halls, that's why Capt. Snell rescued me, and said, 'Why are you there? I've built a theatre. Come to my theatre!'

I learned all my dancing on the Island, was taught by Mr Bellingdon Clerk who was a wonderful teacher and I qualified on Hayling Island. I was the first Hayling Islander – they'd hardly heard of it in London – to gain my finals, which enabled me to teach, put letters after my name. It was the Hayling Island School of the Royal Academy of Dancing, of which wonderful Dame Margot was, in my days, our president.

I started the school just really for people who'd come back from the war; in those days in Hayling there was only the Brownies and their schooling. I had the school for forty years. Very successful it was too, so I'm very proud of that. My mother and my father would get my children from school when I was teaching.

Beryl, Lady Mackworth, born 1915

Portsmouth High School

Then my daughter went to the Portsmouth High School, which meant she went by bus and then train to Portsmouth and walked to Southsea to school, from the Guildhall. The boys both eventually went to Petersfield, to Churcher's College.

Mrs A., born 1920

The Barn Theatre, the original home of the Hayling Island Amateur Dramatic Society.

Pupils at Hayling council school, 1948. Janet Bocking used this photograph to contact her schoolmates for a reunion in 1998: 'Fifty years after I'd been in this particular class,' she says, 'about thirty turned up'.

Walking to School Together

I went to school when I were five. There was only one council school, Mill Rythe.

A lot of people on Hayling went to school with me. We got a season ticket. If it was very bad, we kept to the bus but we usually walked two and a half miles because we looked for birds' nests.

In the summer you were talking all the time about everything around you, the kids were. First of all we picked up Margaret and Lynda Banks, then we went for my cousin Alan, the Jones children, the Donnelly children, Mossy, the Beckett children, Bobby Goddard, Johnny Beck, Alf Dollery, and we picked up at the Yew Tree and we all walked together an' all walked together home, you see.

Noel Pycroft, born 1928

Christmas Choirboys

I worked at the Choir School for eight years an' they pulled that down. We had a lovely church there. We had 140 children. I was the breakfast lady, I worked 6 a.m. to 10 a.m. But then they built all those houses on it. I left the Choir School about 1994. Fr Whitehead was very nice. It was a lovely school. They looked after the children well, boarders aged about four to sixteen or seventeen. And the choir was beautiful, y'know? The singing from the children! They went all over the place, to Italy to see the Pope even. People would ask, specially at Christmas, could the choirboys come? Christmas morning, I gave them their breakfast, then their mums and dads came and picked them up and they all went off for their two weeks' holiday.

Mrs Lilian Townsend-Holmes, born 1930

From School to Service

I left school, I passed the labour exam. I went to Emsworth church school, then when this exam came up, in Fairfield – it was Havant High School then. I walked from Emsworth to the school because our grandmother had gone to visit her sister and there was nobody in the house to give me a halfpenny or a penny for a bus fare. I passed, so I left school at thirteen, and from then I went into service.

Mrs Queenie Gates, born 1903

Suntrap Star-Gazing

My neighbour worked at the Suntrap School and was keen to take the pupils out star-gazing.

Mrs A., born 1920

Suntrap School

I lived in at Suntrap Convalescent School as a probationer nurse in 1935. I quite enjoyed that. It was roughly half asthma cases and half orthopaedic. The doctor in charge of Lord Mayor Treloar hospital, Alton, whose seaside branch was Sandy Point Hospital, used, each Sunday, to visit his orthopaedic patients, who had been sent to Sandy Point to recuperate after their operations. Then he would come to us, to see anyone that we were concerned about; he also used to keep an eye on our orthopaedic patients. Dr A.J. May used to look after us all, patients as well.

Suntrap had about a dozen staff. Sister and Matron, the only trained staff, trained the others. Two years in a hospital like the Suntrap counted for one year of general nursing training then. I was sixteen when I came to the Island and after two years was old enough to enter training hospital.

Mrs Joyce Poore (née Nichol), born 1919

Life at the Suntrap School

I had contracted whooping cough and double pneumonia and was in hospital over the Christmas of 1952. They were going to send me to Hayling Island, to Suntrap. I was told it was owned by Uxbridge and Harrow. I suppose when you are seven years old, you just accept things. On the coach I sat next to some young chap, and I was told if he felt

Brian Shorthouse at the entrance to the Suntrap convalescent home.

43

Having fun on the boating lake at Hayling: Brian Shorthouse's brother comes to visit him at the Suntrap.

ill I was to tell the supervisor. It was me had to ask for a sick bag!

Arriving at Suntrap, I can remember a wooden floor and the smell of polish. Whenever I smell a newly polished floor, it always reminds me of that entrance to Suntrap. At one point, we had to go back into the main building, there was a trapdoor in the floor, and I know I was just with the boys. We had to go down these steps. At the bottom it smelled like a clothing shop. And I was given a pair of boots – lace-up, sort of ankle boots. I was also given pyjamas, possibly shirts, underwear. Why we were given those, why we didn't take them with us, I just don't know. Later on, we were taken over to the school to meet our teachers. The first class we went into was run by a Mr Coombes.

I was very shy. All infants and new intakes were called five o'clockers. They had to be called in at five o'clock for their evening meal and then go to bed. The older pupils went in to evening meal at seven o'clock.

Mr Coombes wore a hearing-aid. In his class we were always given bundles of plain paper that we had to cut up, different sizes, and make notepads. Quite often, instead of giving the notepad back, I would hide it and take it out. They were used for writing, scribbling, drawing. He kept them locked away in the cupboard. A Miss Lee, who dressed in black, was white-haired and rode an old-fashioned bike to school, with a basket on the front. Mr Coombes was very nice, because I never remember him shouting. A Mr Richards, or Richardson, used to shout a lot. Miss Lee let us sit round in little groups while she read a book. I cannot remember writing anything down or learning conventional subjects. Miss Richardson taught country dancing.

In the dining-room, the children had to show their plates to a supervisor who would often send them back to eat more. Dark-coloured meat with yellow fat, very few people believed me, but I am absolutely 100% sure it was horsemeat.

Mr Fielon was more frightening than Mr Upfold. Once, in the dining-hall he said, 'No talking!' He saw me talking and with the back of his hand and almighty strength cuffed me across the back of the neck. Evening meals were more like a high tea, if you didn't have kippers you had baked beans or spaghetti on toast.

On my eighth birthday I was allowed to choose about eight friends to sit at my table. The Suntrap provided a cake plus jelly, ice-cream and sandwiches.

Brian Shorthouse, born 1945

Hoping to go Home Soon

I went to Suntrap in the October of 1952 and was there just over nine months. I can't ever remember any of the boys crying, certainly not juniors or seniors. But at one time, probably only a month after I'd been there, I put my thumb and middle finger of one hand round the wrist of another and said to my friends, 'Look, I've put on all that much weight, I can't close my thumb and finger!' and hoped that I would be going home soon. But it was not to be.

Each dormitory held roughly sixteen. My ward was the junior. We had to strip our beds in the morning, make them with hospital corners. If the supervisors were not satisfied, they had to be done again. I

Pupils and staff of the Suntrap convalescent home. Joyce Poore (second nurse from the left, back row) has fond memories of the school during a more compassionate regime than Brian Shorthouse experienced.

Suntrap boys standing to attention, with Brian Shorthouse on the left in the back row.

helped the other boys, but I never won the prize of a little toy given each week for bed making.

About once a week, the boys had baths in a little room with four or five baths in, one of which was on legs, and you queued up until the supervisor told you you could get in. I can only remember Mr Upfold and Mr Fielding bathing us. Miss Groves or Miss Richardson used to see us into bed each night. Once in bed there was strictly no talking. Mr Upfold or Mr Fielding would walk up and down the dormitories listening for any noise, any whispering.

The boys dormitories had no curtains. The girls' did. But woe betide any boy who was caught anywhere near the girls' dormitories!

There were boys, probably girls as well, they used to call 'drainers'. They had to go into the clinic every morning. I remember seeing them bent over backwards over an 'A' frame, and they had tin mugs and had to try and cough up the sputum and put that into the mug. Every now and again, we had to go for a medical check-up done by the Sister and the nurse: basically, height, weight, and they looked in your eyes and mouth. The usual procedure was to go into an ante-room, get undressed to your underpants and when the Sister was ready, she would boom out, 'Come in'. We had to file in and stand in line and as you reached the Sister she would do the examination. One time, one of the boys had opened the door between the ante-room and the clinic room and he'd seen three girls sitting on the bed they had there. We were a bit perturbed about this and making a bit of a noise and Sister came

Joyce Poore with pupils at the Suntrap in the 1930s. Her husband's home was Coast Guard Cottages.

Janet Bocking's mother, Eileen Stanhoft, with a patient at Suntrap, 1933.

storming in, told us to be quiet and file in. And there we were, in a various array of underpants and the girls, who were probably fourteen or fifteen-year-olds, would not stop giggling. We weren't very happy about this, none of us. We were making a bit of a noise I s'pose; and then Sister shouted out, 'If you boys do not behave, I will make you take your underpants down in front of these girls!' I've never forgotten that and, oh, I wish I could meet that Sister now and tell her exactly what I thought of her!'

Once a week, when we became seven o'clockers, or even eight o'clockers, we filed into the hall and were given a film show. I remember Gary Cooper in *Distant Drums*, that was one of the best films I had ever seen. Miss Richardson took us for Sunday walks, over the creeks. A main path ran through, with rivulets running off, which we liked jumping over.

The Matron wasn't very tall but she looked tall to me. She was always upright, walked in a sort of military fashion, wore a big, white head-dress, was very authoritative. But every now and again, she came round the ward to have a little chat with us and she would always give you a little cuddle and was rather nice.

Brian Shorthouse, born 1945

CHAPTER 5

Love and Marriage

Grace Townsend marries her first husband Sgt Arthur Spencer of the RAF in 1941.

An Anniversary to Remember

Dieppe, when we tried to invade and the whole sea was just covered in boats, mostly Navy, and the planes were just coming over, that day it was my first wedding anniversary, it was August 1942.

We used to have a searchlight round the back here and they used to try to bomb the searchlight. It must have been about 20 August – I went down to the post office, that's how I happened to see them.

I wanted to visit my husband in Lincoln on Bomber Command. These planes were coming over and firing, and I ran down the garden to the air-raid shelter and I had the bullets all round me. Anyway, that night I went up to Lincoln. I was only just, not eighteen, I crossed London on my own. It was my wedding anniversary. You know how romantic you are when you're just about that age? Anyway, my husband wouldn't let me stay. He said if he didn't come back one night, what would happen? And he didn't come back, he was a prisoner of war for three years. He came back in 1945, but was only in England for six months and he was killed on the railway. It was appalling. I was a widow at twenty-one. There was no work about, so he went on the railway tracks. I married again, but since I've lost my husband a few years ago, it's all come back. It's funny the way the men go, and it's the widows are left, isn't it?

Mrs Grace Townsend, born 1924

Dancing on the Pier

There were two ballrooms at South Parade Pier, 2s 6d to go in. In those days, you went to a dance, you never thought about beer, you had a cup of tea. It was about the fourth time we went I found out where the bar was! I went for the dancing. Foxtrot, quickstep, tango – that was what's called dancing. This shaking and shuffling – you don't have to learn anything. I went to night-school for two years to learn dancing.

On leaving the Royal Marines, I went back home to Brum. We was together, just courting. I used to come down from Birmingham for the weekend; used to tell my mum I was going to see a mate! Yes, it cost me £2 0s 8d return fare, Birmingham to here.

John Plimbley, 1927-1999

Land Girl Weds

I met my husband, a Royal Marine, at a dance at South Parade Pier, Southsea. I left the Land Army to get married.

Mrs Ivy Plimbley (née Wakely)

Land girl Ivy Wakely, seen here at Ham Farm, became Mrs Plimbley.

Alice and Bessie Derben (on the right) in the postal service during the First World War.

To Bess, Love Jack

Big Aunt Bess was a sad lady because she certainly was engaged to be married; when she died, all she left was a little brown piece of paper saying 'killed in action' or 'missing presumed killed' from the First World War. She never spoke about it and she never married. This was posted to Aunt Bess when she was still living at the Tournebury brickyard: 28 November 1916 from the Field Service. She didn't leave any letters, but she obviously wanted us to know that she'd had somebody: 'I am quite well. Letter follows. Jack.'

Mrs Janet Bocking, born 1939

Keeping Mum

Father was a builders' merchant based at West Town, opposite the West Town Hotel. He branched away from the hotel because

there wasn't enough business there to keep my mother, you know, when he got married. Mother got married to him in 1932, and he started the Hayling Coal and Transport Company.

Michael Camp, born 1933

Happy on Hayling

We both come from Portsmouth. My husband worked in the dockyard drawing office. He was a shipwright apprentice when I first knew him. He served in the RAF as a navigator and we married in 1946.

Mrs Joan McAndrew, born 1925

Sparkes' Boat-Yard

We had many friends, mostly my brothers' friends, down at Mengham, known to us as 'the Creek', and that's where I really learned about boats. In the mud – and it was wonderful. So I spent many years there and I met my first husband through sailing, which I eventually did at Hayling Island Sailing Club at Mengham, as it was then. My first husband taught me all about sailing. He was a great sailing man, Bib Sparkes, yes, and of course my two daughters are Sparkes. And I was very very grateful to him, all my life I have been.

He and I built Sparkes' Boat-Yard. We were rather sort of Captain Scotts. When the Sailing Club was built, he was then in charge of a very large yacht, which was kept here on Hayling – *Viking* – she cruised everywhere but he was looking after her but realized the Sailing Club ought to have a boat-yard handy. So we said, 'Ooh, yes, let's start a boat-yard!' and we found the plot and we stuck a stick in and found the owner. The owner put up the money, because we hadn't got any, and this so-called Sandy Point Estate was one big field owned by Farmer Tickner. The gentleman who put up the money for the boat-yard had also bought this estate, so he said, 'Well, now, if you're going to have a boat-yard here, you'll need a house. You'd better have this house.' Well, it's a very good plot!

So then, sadly, my first husband was killed, on the Island, on his motorbike. In those days they didn't wear crash-helmets. Which was very sad. For me, especially my daughters, and they were about eight and five I think, yes.

Beryl, Lady Mackworth, born 1915

Moving to Magdala Road

I came to live in Hayling, 1948. We moved into this house, Magdala Road, June 1949. Married in the February. We lived in rooms

The boat-yard at Hayling Island Sailing Club.

– Kings Road and all that wasn't built, it was all fields. The only places you could rent was Elm Grove Estate, little bungalows there, or Seafront Estate.

John Plimbley, 1927-1999

Working Together

We were married at Fareham Registry Office then moved back here. We both used to work at Plessey's.

Roy Chamberlain, born 1929

Born on the Outbreak of War

We lived in Hayling since before the war but we lived in Portsmouth first because my husband was in the Navy. I have two sons, Colin, who lives in Kensington, who was born practically the first day of the Second World War because the shock brought it on – I didn't know where my husband was – and John, about eighteen months older.

Mrs Beryl Bonniface

Friday Night Dances

I came to start a nursing career in 1935 and of course I married and I still stayed on the Island, at North Hayling. In those days, you had to make your own fun; there was quite a lot doing on Hayling. The Hut in St Leonard's Avenue had Friday night dances we all went to, and I made friends with Hayling people. We used to go out to them, and of course I met my husband when he was on the building of

the new Suntrap and my bosom buddy that started the same day as I did at Suntrap and came from Wales, her husband was a Hayling chap. We four went out together and played tennis. They stayed on the Island till her husband was called up for the war and she went back to Wales and I got married and stayed on Hayling. I was married at Gosport, March 1939. My husband's home was at Coast Guard Cottages.

Mrs Joyce Poore (née Nichol), born 1919

Whistling for the Children

My husband and his family knew Hayling, having had various houses from springtime to autumn; they knew the family of Pembroke Cross, agent for Warren Sands Estate, and that is how we came to live on Hayling, in March 1946.

It was like living in a wood – there were these trees all the way round and fields. I was expecting my third child. Bringing up children on the Island was wonderful, because it was very safe, and enclosed. They could walk to play on the beach or in the fields. My husband made them a tree-house in the corner by the front gate. I had a stable-door to my kitchen and when they were playing on the beach, I would whistle, and they would come!

Mrs A., born 1920

Escaping the Depression

I had two good friends worked near me in Portsmouth and we always had the same time off so we would gang up and meet on our Sunday half-days, go to concerts on the pier. I worked there quite a while, then met a boy-friend. He was a Scotsman, I married him in 1926. He was in the Argyll and Sutherland Highlanders.

We lived in Stirling Castle for a bit. Then he left the Army at the worst time possible, when the Depression was on. We came back, about 1934, to Hayling. My dad was living in Hayling. We lived with my stepmother for a while in Elm Grove, in the council houses – eventually we got our own place, in Rails Lane, a little flint cottage and the biggest spiders I ever saw! It belonged to Mr Jim Hedger, the farmer. Then we moved to the corner of Legion Lane, it's a shop now but it was a lovely little cottage. Belonged to a butcher, he used to give us a nice joint of beef every Christmas, providing he could cut the holly in the front garden.

Mrs Queenie Gates, born 1903

Watching the World Go By

I was fourteen. I came back to London with my mother, and from then on I've had three husbands, and I've just three lovely children – yes, two boys and one girl – they're all workin' on the Island, got their own homes and everything. So they're all doin' fine.

In 1952, I came to Hayling with my first husband's sister, to stay at Eastoke and I had my two little children then, and my husband was workin' in East Africa so I stayed on 'cos I loved it so much, and I've never gone back. I eventually moved to Norfolk Crescent. I lived seven years down in the basement of No. 41, and twenty-one years in my balcony flat. Nearly forty years I lived at the Crescent. Me and my late husband used to sit on the balcony and watch all the holiday people. There was loads of people, it was beautiful.

Mrs Lilian Townsend-Holmes, born 1930

Dancing and Destiny

It's rather funny actually. I had a friend who wanted to learn ballroom dancing. Not my scene at all, not that period. I was sixteen. But he didn't have the courage to go, so he dragged me along to a place in Portsmouth and I met my wife, Catherine, there that night. I never went again, but we stayed together and eventually got married. I mean, if he hadn't have dragged me along, we'd never have met. Because I only ever went there once, I've never been a ballroom dancer. I just went to help a friend out!

Eric Dossetter, born 1942

Always With Me

I don't mind being alone. All the people who have been with me all my life are still here, with me. I wrote a poem about him being just behind the door, for I feel he's here. And he was such a positive, definite person he couldn't have lived doing nothing. He went on a committee, access for the handicapped, after a series of strokes.

Mrs Joan Duckett, 1915-1999

TOLL BRIDGE AND LANGSTONE HARBOUR, HAYLING ISLAND

The Old Bridge: the toll bridge and Langstone Harbour.

The Old Road Bridge

I went to school with Noel Pycroft. We used to go winkling together. We'd walk to Havant and sell the winkles for a shilling to a Havant shop, spend all our money as like as not, then they wouldn't let us over the bridge; used to take our matches or something for the toll.

Lawrence Shepherd, born 1927

A Balloon for the Toll Man

It was the Old Bridge, not the one that is now. And the bus was too heavy so you had to get off, walk across and then get on at the other side and of course there was a toll man. When I was in my late teens, we used to come back from Southsea in a little car and we didn't want to pay the ninepence for the toll man, so we waited until ten o'clock when he went in, to get his drink in the pub, and then we just came across. One day, I tied a balloon on that gate and, with my lipstick I wrote: 'We owe you 9d' or whatever it was.

Mrs Brenda Wood, born 1915

A Friendly Bus Ride Home

As passengers from the bus to or from Havant, we had to disembark to walk over the Old Bridge. Everyone was friendly and a good comradeship was often formed.

Arnold Sharples
Former Leading Seaman

'Avant for 'Ayling Hisland!

I remember how beautiful our surroundings were in the fine summer weather. On leaving or returning to the Island we always had to walk across the bridge, which was thought to be unsafe. There was an unmistakable voice of the porter at Havant station who announced the arrival of every train: 'Avant for 'Ayling Hisland!'

Martin Loft
Former Corporal, Royal Marines
attached to MOLCAB Unit 4
stationed on Hayling 1944-1945

Bus Ride to Night-School

It was fourpence return from Manor Road council houses to Havant. I used to go to night-school in Portsmouth three nights a week. We used to have to get off the bus, rain, sleet or snow, and walk the bridge. There was always a crowd of us that were going to college. We used to have to pay for

Langstone railway swing bridge open for shipping.

doing our own education then. It was for my electrical qualifications. From sixteen onwards it was Monday, Wednesday and Friday evenings at college.

Colin Vaughn, born 1932

Five Ton Limit

The trouble was, before they built the New Bridge they were restricted with the weight you could take over the Old Bridge, so you could only really bring I think it was a maximum of 5 tons which included the weight of the lorry.

Michael Camp, born 1933

Off the Buses

As the New Bridge was being built, it was terrible on the Old Bridge. My daughter left home each morning at 8 a.m. for Petersfield High School for Girls, by bus from Northney to Havant, then by train from Havant station.

Only six passengers were allowed to ride the bus over the weak Old Bridge; the rest had to walk over, and it was always the schoolchildren that had to get off so she was very frustrated.

Mrs Joyce Poore (née Nichol), born 1919

Lay-by, Half-Way

I always went across in the car or on the motorbike. But I had to pay the toll: sixpence.

There was a lay-by half-way across for a passing place. As far as I can remember, I never saw the Old Bridge raised. The water was deep enough for the boats to come through.

Roy Skennerton, born 1920

Sheltered by the Bus

If it was raining, the bus used to drive slowly and you used to walk on the lee side.

Roy Chamberlain, born 1929

Red and Green Oil for the Lamp

My children were indignant that, when crossing the Old Bridge, they had to get out and walk, while holiday-makers remained in the bus, sometimes when it was dark, raining and blowing hard. It seemed a long journey across in such conditions. The toll keeper regulated the flow of traffic by turning a lantern which showed red or green, to signal 'stop' or 'go'. He told the children that he used red and green oil. They would ask him, 'Have you got green oil in your lamp tonight?' as they waited to walk across.

Mrs A., born 1920

All Winds and Weathers

I had to be at work at 7 a.m., at a Langstone factory, behind the Ship Inn. We had to get off the bus all winds and weathers and walk over the bridge; it was so crazy because the Army just used to drive everything. We used to have some dreadful rows, it could be blowing a gale – you'd almost get blown away.

Mrs Grace Townsend, born 1924

A Bus Overloaded with Marines

In 1945 I started working for two years on the Island. The buses were small 26-seater vehicles because the bridge would not take any heavier. With so many Army and naval camps during the war, the buses used to get very full, and 26 seats were not a lot when you have a lot of heavy servicemen. One occasion, coming back from Hayling to Havant, we got as far as Hayling School, now the junior school, there was a former holiday camp just by it. There were Marines in it, and we stopped at the stop there. The conductress was standing with her back to the driver's partition at the front of the bus and these Marines kept coming and coming. The rules were that you had 26 people seated and I think a total of 8 standing. However, we left on that occasion with 26 people standing. When we got to the road bridge one of the two men in charge of it, a toll bridge, was a Mr Budd. He had an Army type moustache and was a stickler for the rules, so the conductress, who couldn't move – so many of the chaps had got on the bus she didn't collect many fares – said to all the Marines, 'Please try and find somebody's lap to sit on!' while we went over the bridge, so that Mr Budd wouldn't see there were so many people on this overloaded vehicle.

A.A.F. Bell, born 1927

The Opening of the New Bridge

Well, I was working when the New Bridge was opened but I remember my mother and her sister went out on a day trip the day there was the parade of veteran cars.

Mrs Mavis Chamberlain (née Tucker),
1936-2000

The New Bridge, tolls freed at last.

CHAPTER 7

The Hayling Billy

The Hayling Billy, a Terrier engine, works each summer for the Isle of Wight Railway Company Ltd, Haverstreet, Isle of Wight. (photograph: the Isle of Wight Railway Company Ltd)

Learning to Fire the Engine

As a boy, I remember the coaches had red seats with black buttons, ex-London and South Western coaches, no corridor but each compartment had its own toilet. The engines were always smaller in height than the coaches. Tall chimneys.

In 1946 I became friendly with one of the drivers on the train and he taught me how to fire the engine. I built up a friendship which lasted for much longer than that period.

A.A.F. Bell, born 1927

Senior porters Alf Ripsher and Ray Woolgar, Signalman Doug Todd and Relief Signalman Herbert Brook at Hayling Island station, 26 October 1963. (photograph: A.A.F. Bell)

To School on the Hayling Billy

I went to Churcher's College, Petersfield, when I was just about eleven, by Hayling train then the train from Havant to Petersfield. Of course, we still had the air raids.

Michael Camp, born 1933

The Beaches are Wired Off

From Bedhampton, as a boy, I used to come down to a friend's beach hut. We used to travel by train to Havant, go over the railway bridge and onto the Hayling train. A long walk down Staunton Avenue to the beach. We didn't go to Hayling during wartime because it was a protected area and the beaches were all wired off.

A.A.F. Bell, born 1927

Engine in the Car Park

The pub Hayling Billy was built after the train stopped [the last passenger service was in 1963]. The train engine was in the pub car park, before it went off to the Isle of Wight.

Ernie Turner, born 1943

The Railway in Wartime

Petrol was rationed, we used to go by bicycle. It wasn't easy to get around, but we had the railway of course.

Col. John D'E Coke RM, born 1916

Held Up at the Level Crossing

Oh, yes, there was the Hayling Billy, we didn't use it much because we had the cars, it was an inconvenience in a way, inasmuch as they used to cause such tailbacks at weekends at the level crossing [Langstone]. There were one or two people commuted, they used to get on the Hayling Billy to Havant and then go up to London.

Mrs Hazel Warner, born 1929

The Railway Closes

The railway, I think, closed in 1963, didn't it?

This chap was going to take over and run a tramcar along the railway line, I don't know what happened to that idea. Hayling Light Transit. I don't think it could get any support.

Michael Camp, born 1933

Fred Norris with North Star, the North Hayling halt oil lamp, at Hayling station. (photograph: A.A.F. Bell)

Ray Woolgar in the ticket-office at Hayling Island station on 26 October 1963. (photograph: A.A.F. Bell)

The Birth of the Station Theatre

We were at the Barn Theatre, which was owned by Mr and Mrs Selby; they were getting on in years – both we and they were concerned about what was going to happen to the theatre when they passed on. They were in their seventies then. It was unlikely the estate would continue as it was and if it had to be sold then the Hayling Island Amateur Dramatic Society [HIADS] would lose the Barn. So we were in a bit of a quandary what to do. At that time, I was vice-chairman of the society. We decided to talk to Mr Selby, and say, 'We really think we must think about our future, we've no wish to leave, but obviously...' They were

quite understanding, they were concerned about it as well.

I should make it clear that the society had used the Barn Theatre from its conception in 1948, totally rent-free, which was marvellous; so in December of 1992 we had a dinner, I was with a few other members and what we were going to do came up. I said, 'Well, what about the old engine shed?' That's what it actually is. It's shoebox in shape.

Then of course there was no way HIADS could finance that sort of project. At that time the Lottery had just set up, so we decided we would have a big fund-raising, then approach the Lottery. That went through the HIADS committee in the January and we started from that.

Fred Norris and G. Install, guards at Hayling Island station. (photograph: A.A.F. Bell)

Taxi-driver Stevenson waits for fares at Hayling Island station with his Austin Metropolitan LLL 27 (photograph: A.A.F. Bell)

At the same time I took over as chairman of the society. I set up this Chairman's Project and we went from there. What's really remarkable about it was the enormous support we got from the people of Hayling. Virtually every organization: church-based, businessmen, whatever. We had, I don't know how many hundreds of events, from filling Smartie tubes through jumble sales to book sales, plant sales, and we raised an enormous sum of money, really, for a small island. Something like £50,000 ourselves. I was county councillor for the Island so I thought, 'Let's try some friends of the county council' and Fred Emery Wallace was chairman of the council at the time, he was always a good friend of the arts, so I phoned

him and he said he would support it, put it to the county council and they actually gave us our first £20,000. The actual engine shed, the land, was the property of the Havant borough council. And again, talking to the borough council, if they could see we could make it viable, show them our business plan, they would support us. And they did, right throughout the project. So we got the theatre site at a peppercorn rent, £25 yearly lease, so long as it's viable. And it is, very much so. It made a great profit this year, we can invest in more equipment. The first two years we averaged about 86% seats filled!

We had a very good local architect, Crichley. He'd just started in Havant then and was quite interested in doing something that was different. We had to put it out to tender, the first phase, we used a company in Havant for making the existing building waterproof, actually re-roofing. The second part, which was the largest, all the new building, was carried out by Hayling Builders, Station Road.

Capt. Derek Oakley MBE, RM produced a video, which took the project right the way through to completion, as an archive, actually, of the building of the the theatre.

Virtually everyone in the society worked on the theatre although, obviously, the main building was done professionally. All the painting, building of the seating, stage: we put in tens of thousands of man-hours. It took us five years; we'd thought it would take eight. We finished in 1998. So we were within our time-scale and we finished within the budget as well.

And what I haven't mentioned, of course, was that we had a considerable sum from the Lottery, we had two lots. The Foundation for Sports and Arts gave us £40,000. That account paid for the car park surfacing. If you worked out all the money that went in and a reasonable estimate of all the man-hours that we put in, we reckon the project would have cost over £1.5 million. It really is very good value for money when you look at what's there. We were using it before we'd finished.

I have heard it said, at the beginning, 'All that money, why couldn't HIADS use the Community Centre?' But we actually, as of now, don't have enough time for all the visiting things that want to come, our own productions and all the other things that we do. The Station Theatre is used fifty-two weeks a year, six days a week, it's

The previously derelict Hayling Island station building formed the core of the Station Theatre, now the home of the Hayling Island Amateur Dramatic Society (HIADS). Work on the building was completed in 1998.

Capt. Derek Oakley MBE, RM, president of HIADS, is interviewed about the opening of the new Station Theatre. The theatre has risen like a phoenix from the flames of the ruined old station.

never empty. So there's no way we could do all of that in the Community Centre because they're very busy themselves. And we have a state of the art lighting and sound system, and virtually every group we've had there have said the venue's fantastic. If you go back to the old recital rooms, it's about the same size and shape, the classic shape for recitals, that's why the acoustics are so good.

A lot of people on Hayling have a long background of interest in theatre – we've also got a number of members who were on the stage professionally in their younger years and some of the youngsters are excellent. One of the last things I did was *Cold Comfort Farm*, we had every generation working together. So you'll see youngsters of about ten or twelve, even young teenagers, chatting away with people in their seventies with no inhibitions at all, because of their common interests. It works very well.

Eric Dossetter, born 1942

CHAPTER 8

The Holiday Business

Highworth Caravan Camp.

The Holiday Season

Dick Cleave started the largest caravan site on the Island. Caravan sites were at first used for holidays, the same people revisited repeatedly. They would retire to the Island, their children followed them and started businesses. They say you can buy anything you like on the Island. The number of shops increased as more people came to live here, but they depend, as do the hotels and bed and breakfasts, on the length of the holiday season, which used to be eighteen weeks.

Now it's six or seven. Hotels are few: Broadoak, Cocklewarren Cottage, the Rook Hollow, in Church Road, and the Posthouse. The Newtown Manor was originally a big house.

Mrs Dorothy S. Millns, born 1943

Railway Accommodation

I stayed in a railway carriage, with a friend, for a while; it said 'No Smoking' on the

An Eastoke bungalow with a railway carriage extension. Could this carriage have been one of those let as holiday accommodation?

wooden doors! Just proper carriages, called Shanty Town. Summer accommodation. People could stay there in winter, however, a lot of them didn't 'cos the sea used to come right the way over. Over the Beach Club as well, the tides were pretty high.

Mrs Lilian Townsend-Holmes, born 1930

The First Holiday Camp

I was not involved in running the holiday camps; I mean, not officially. I used to obviously take an interest. Nowadays, on expensive cruises, the activities are basically the same. People were entertained, used to join in with everything, put on their own shows, it was like a big family, really. At the end of the week, everyone knew everyone else. They used to always enjoy it. Oh, they used to come back again, bring their children down, it was very much a family holiday; and then when the children grew up they used to come back with their children.

Before my husband was born, my father-in-law owned the land down where the fun-fair was; there was a house in the middle there, he sold that to Bill Butlin to build a fun-fair and with the proceeds he then started the first holiday camp, about 1928. They had the nice little wooden chalets. Well, now they are far too sophisticated. Completely altered. Oh, the Navy had the whole lot during the war. They took them over.

It was very much a family business. They used to have silly shows like knobbly knees; the men used to dress as women, which was

A Guide and Handbook

HAYLING ISLAND

THE HAPPY ISLE

SANDS OF DELIGHT
LAND OF HEALTH
~ & ENJOYMENT ~

Second Edition

AUTHENTIC MAP, ILLUSTRATIONS
DESCRIPTIVE NOTES
HISTORICAL INCIDENTS, GENERAL INFORMATION

1/-

Published by

GREENS HAYLING BEACH CAFÉS LTD

The Sands, Hayling Island.

Boats in Chichester Harbour off Sandy Point.

A hat competition at the Coronation Holiday Camp, 1957. Audrey Cozens is on the left.

hilarious in those days, nothing ever nasty about it. But they had ballroom dancing, every night. And the thing that parents liked, they always had people would arrange things for the children, so the parents were completely relaxed. I think they used to have a patrol, before the days of radio. You would tell somebody where the baby was, and then, later on they did have, at Sinah, the radio and they could switch it on and see if there was a baby howling.

I used to do odd things, when we were opening new camps. The idea was, a week's holiday was going to be a week's wages of an average worker, I mean, it was amazing, the whole business that they could have a holiday there. Everything was provided; drinks weren't. They didn't have to go off the camp, didn't particularly want to, either. It was so booked out that, on the first of January, sacksful of mail used to come. And now, down Sinah, they have their own self-contained en suite chalets. They don't have any children now – mostly retired. I think people mostly who are free to go are retired people.

Mrs Hazel Warner, born 1929

Chalets and Sea-Walls

I've worked here since 1974. I'm Maintenance Manager now; came as an electrician, worked as assistant to the previous manager, up until around 1990 when he retired, and I continued with his job. It was called Sunshine Holiday Camp. Warner's changed the name to Mill Rythe.

We're a fully catered site. It's changed – they were little wooden shacks, which just had a wash-hand basin in them, outside toilet blocks, outside shower rooms, much the same as if you were on a camping holiday in a tent.

Who will be Miss Sunshine 1964?

We used to take, in the 1970s, when the chalets were like that, 1,100 people. But when we started putting in bathrooms, rooms disappeared because one room became two bathrooms. We now take 600 to 650 people.

A chalet, anything that goes wrong in a house goes wrong there. You imagine, 259 chalets – there's 259 bathrooms and no end of extra wash-hand basins, so plumbing-wise there's a lot of work. Electric-wise there's a lot of work with replacing of light bulbs and light fittings.

We have a great big open field down the other end of the camp. The water goes all the way round us. A sea-bank wall round the outside, you can walk around. I've never known it to flood. There is a bund which goes across the farmer's field to the highest point on Hayling which is just outside, before Tournebury. If the sea got through the sea-wall, the bund is supposed to stop the water from coming any further. We've had all these flood warnings over the last two years; we watched, but nothing's happened, and to be honest, if water came in it would run downhill, go right past us.

Ernie Turner, born 1943

Changing Hands

When I first came to the Sunshine, the film *Confessions of a Holiday Camp* was made here. Yeah, and I worked with the crews supplying their electric supplies. We've had several television shows done from here, holiday programmes; we had an Esther Rantzen, *Heart of Gold*, and conferences. It's an enjoyable time although you are having to work hard.

Before my time, the Sunshine was privately owned by local businessmen, mainly Mr G.A. Day of Portsmouth. In 1971, Rank's went into it in a big way. And they sold it to Warner's:1986, it was owned

A crowded beach at the height of the summer.

by Grand Metropolitan, who owned Warner's at the time, then, I think about 1990 or 1991, Rank bought them back. So we've got back into being Rank again. We became Haven-Warner. Now Mill Rythe has provision for children, and became Haven, one of Rank's larger subsidiaries.

Ernie Turner, born 1943

Changing Times

I collect these holiday brochures; you can see since 1967 provision for visitors changed as public expectations changed. All the rooms have television. The reading and writing room is now a laundrette; the swimming-pool is all one depth.

We used to have a motor boat which took people for free rides down to the harbour entrance, there was riding tuition, morning tea as well. They still had maid service. We used to have an intercom so that parents could hear their children – we don't do that any more. That was a rented thing, so if there was something went wrong with it we couldn't lay our hands on it.

Ernie Turner, born 1943

Holidays for a Lifetime

The sandy beach was very popular; my uncle and aunt from near Epsom came down all of their married life, right up to, even in the war they got a permit to come. Loads of people did, that's why Hayling's grown, and then they'd bring their children.

Mrs Grace Townsend, born 1924

Caravans in Bloom

The Oven Campsite, in its very early days, was nearly all tents. At St Herman's site, we used to have our gipsy caravan there, in the entrance. It was floodlit – it used to look rather nice.

The beaches used to be absolutely packed. Fashions change. People go abroad so much. Some of these caravans are still there. They're a bit old now – they last longer than ten years if people look after them. I used to run a garden competition for gardens and roses for people who hired the sites to encourage them to look after their gardens. We had the shop at St Herman's, then.

My mother gave up the garden competition, because it got a bit sort of

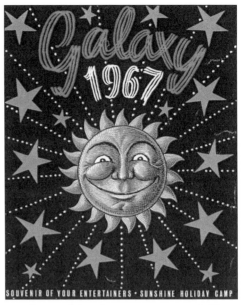

Sunshine Holiday Camp programme, 1967.

Michael Camp with his gipsy caravan.

tense. We had one chap there who had nothing in his garden the night before, and the day of the competition it was a mass of blooms! He put all of these geraniums down in boxes, and of course he didn't get a prize because he hadn't grown them and we got more trouble!

Michael Camp, born 1933

Caravan Sites on the Island

We first had caravans at St Herman's, down at Southwood Road, the year I was born, about 1933. It was just a meadow then. And of course with the West Town Hotel, people used to come by train and go to the hotel and sort of get their bearings. Two ladies came from somewhere along the South Coast and this caravan site had been closed down and they wanted to bring their caravans to Hayling, so my grandfather thought it was quite a good idea, and it started from there. Gradually we built two toilet blocks and put on water and what have you, and it just sort of took off. Weekend bungalows was the thing in those days. People would come for their holidays and most of the caravans were converted buses or old furniture vans, the only thing that was available then. And of course some touring vans, very flimsy ones, were just beginning to start appearing.

We never had any railway carriages. Caravaning was very basic then, quite different to these very posh £44,000 mobile homes. I run fourteen caravan sites, I think. Some of them are very small; all on Hayling. Little sites at Eastoke, about twelve, Certificated Locations are up here, they're only for Caravan Club members: one here at Lower Tye, one at Gutner and one at Westcroft's on the main road. The others are static sites where people can stay for eight months of the year if they want to.

They are all their own caravans and they rent the pitch from us. They keep them there for years, as long as they want to, and then when they retire and think they'd like to move down from London and live here all the year, we've found that's what the pattern is. London and Reading, the catchment area is, really.

Michael Camp, born 1933

Carnival and Coronation

Warner's used to have excellent carnival floats; they used to travel all around their holiday camps. Yes, Southleigh, Northney, Coronation and Sinah Warren, and latterly the Mill Rythe, which was Sunshine.

The Northney one was up near the

bridge, its been built on, the Sunshine, now Mill Rythe, that's still open. Sinah Warren's in Ferry Road – they spent a lot of money and made a really nice job of it, rebuilding. Then, there's Lakeside, which used to be called the Coronation, at the end of Fishery Lane.

Michael Camp, born 1933

A Summer Bunglow

It was very sort of rural; I remember it round Eastoke which is where my dad built the bungalow. Dad was an estate developer in London and because my mother got fed up with just coming down for the day, she said, 'Can you do something? Can you build a bungalow?' So he bought a plot of land and then we come down for the whole summer. My gran and me, two brothers and Mum and the two dogs and the cat. We used to take up residence and spend our time on the beach. It was lovely. And Dad used to go and work in London all week and then come back at weekends. After the summer holidays were over, we'd pack up and go home. Then we'd come down, during the winter, and a lot of people did that. There were a couple of dentists, one from Devizes – one of his sons still lives in Hollow Lane.

Mrs Mavis Chamberlain (née Tucker), 1936-2000

CHAPTER 9

Work

Unloading gravel from the barge Mab *on to Langstone Quay: Sid Luff, Jim Stride, and Tom Hatchard (?).*

Going to Sea

At fourteen I went to sea as a deck-boy, clean-up boy, wash-up boy, on Admiral Fisher's father's yacht, *Viking*, which I enjoyed, though I got terribly seasick. That's what really got me on going to sea. A lot of people from Hayling went to sea.

Roy Smith, born 1923

Sea-Borne Coal

The Hayling Coal and Transport Company, mainly we used to have sea-borne coal from the East coast, from Keadby in Lincolnshire. We sold the yard to Fred Skipper.

Unloading from the boats, we had wicker baskets and they were wound up with ship's gear. They took about two hundredweight of coal, and then were swung out on a boom

Hayling Coal and Transport's mobile crane and lorry.

from the boat and tipped up into the tip-carts. Then latterly, after the war, when we recommenced getting coal by water, we had a crane there. During the war we got the coal by rail, it was unloaded at the railway station; and when the Hayling Billy closed, then we had it by road. But it was always, historically, cheaper by water. That's why we were a few shillings a ton cheaper.

We used to go down near the ferry and clear all the sand off the roads, every year. It's the Golf Club land, by the gun-site. There was lots and lots of concrete then, for the making of aerodromes, in the war. We used to hire out plant and machinery. We did furniture removals as well. T. Tree Cottage, we knocked down for a builder on the Seafront. It was next to the Olive Leaf, a great shame really. Old fisherman's cottage.

Michael Camp, born 1933

Joining the Family Firm

I came into the family firm which was Hayling Coal and Transport when I finished my National Service and then, of course, the caravan sites which we've got now.

The Camp family has always been interested in horses, so we ran heavy horses right up until the 1960s. The lorries started coming in, the first lorry we had was 1935, but we kept on with the horses for short deliveries. You had to have lorries for the building materials and what have you.

Michael Camp, born 1933

Sparkes' Yard and the Hurricane

After the war, I worked at Sparkes' Boat-Yard, Sandy Point. I thought I would get a seagoing job again, but never did. I stayed at the boat-yard, building and repairs. There's a marina there now. It's a boat-yard still, but not in the same sense that we had it. Slipways and that sort of thing. It's all cranes now.

We made small boats, the famous Sharpie class, and odd motor boats. Mainly the work was maintenance and winter storage. Putting them in the sheds, stowing away the gear. I started in 1947 and left when I retired, 1988. Long time. Very interesting work. I did some salvage work with vessels run ashore, my salvage experience stood me in good stead for recovering boats.

After the hurricane of 1987, about 200 and odd boats in Chichester Harbour were stranded on the beaches. I went over to Thorney Island with our yard launch and two or three hands; we got them all off and those that we couldn't reach had washed up

so far, we got a big crane, craned them up, you know? But it was so thickly along that shore that boats went ashore and others crashed in on top of them. That was a terrible storm.

Roy Smith, born 1923

The Carousel

I've worked in the Carousel, up on Beachlands; the children were small. We used to have the monkeys [Monkey Island] and boats, and on the beach was horses, pedal boats, to hire. It was all so gay and everything. I worked servin' up food – chips and that, sort of chef or cook. My children used to play around, come in and have their dinner with me, you know? Our young son, he was only about seven then, he used to go

Importing coal at Mengham Quay.

Monkey Island and the boating lake, with the Royal Hotel and Norfolk Crescent in the background.

round and take cups of tea to all the stall-holders and earn himself a couple of pennies that way.

Mrs Lilian Townsend-Holmes, born 1930

From Baking to Sail-Making

I was a cook at the Sailing Club, then worked at Price's Bakery, Portsmouth; used to cycle from here, get to work seven o'clock. About eighteen of us used to go over the ferry; dockyard workers and that, the first boat, half past six, do the day's work and then come back. Then I came to Biggs & Barber's on the Island. The bakehouse was up the Seafront, behind that row of cottages. The baker, Fred Viney, used to live in the house with the big lawn. That was in two flats. In the other flat was Reg Bleany, a confectioner at Mengham.

I was a roundsman. Used to do North Hayling, except sometimes, on a Sunday, height of the season, Fred used to come and knock me out of bed. 'Come on,' he said, 'they've run out of bread,' so we had to go and knock a dough up. There was no traffic. I had a motor van on the bakery, we all had vans, motor vans and one electric, 1950-1953.

I had a horse-drawn milk cart, working for Doug Walters' dairy. That little girl, my daughter, was born in 1950. Chichester Dairies bought us up when Dougi Walters died. They got rid of the horses and we come on to the electrics. Because there was only two of us up there that could drive, I had to teach the others to drive the electric floats! You only put the foot on the pedal and went, no gears.

You could have a driving licence just for electric vans. I mean, until 1939, nobody bothered with tests. I've had a car since

1951. I had a couple, and then I had a big Alvis. Long as this room!

Since, I've worked ten years making sails. Field's sail-making place makes beautiful sails for big yachts, exports them.

John Plimbley, 1927-1999

Chambermaid at the Royal Hotel

My mother lived at Purbrook. I came here to work at the Royal Hotel. When there was a decent hotel. They had fun-fairs and things. I was in service, from seventeen. We were paid 15s a week, a good wage in those days because we were kept, you see. That was mainly our pocket-money. But we worked hard. There's all carrying up and down stairs. The linen cupboard used to be in the basement; well, you'd be changing twenty beds and I used to talk to the porters, they used to carry mine up for me.

When I think back, I didn't think anything of it. We had to earn a living. There were waiters and porters, corridor maids, chambermaids; oh, and cooks and chefs. Waiters in the dining-room, not girls in the dining-room. Another thing, hot-water bottles in beds, whoever wanted one. There was a big thing left in the kitchen on the stove and then you had to take the hot-water bottles around. They had vacuum cleaners; but you had to take water up, carry water round at night for washing. So different now, isn't it? I mean you don't see the maid in the bedroom, and you had to work from seven in the morning to ten at night. We were

John Plimbley's milk cart parked outside his Magdala Avenue home. One of these little girls is his daughter.

The Crescent, Hayling Island. The Royal Hotel is the building on the right of the picture, just beyond the elegant sweep of the Crescent.

supposed to have two hours off in the afternoon but of course if I idled a little time away and had to catch up, sometimes we didn't always; and a half day a week, that was all, and I think every other Sunday. It took most of the day to get home on days off.

It was a good hotel; they came specially for the golf. You couldn't join the golf club, the likes of you or me perhaps, but you've got to be sort of very different, but they did say that Charlie Chaplin and people like that had stayed there. It was very hard work in those days.

Mrs Eva Prior, born 1910

The Farmers' Market

I'd just started work, break of war, because I used to walk along the road and watch the

planes comin' over. I'm seventy-three now and I started work when I was fourteen.

I used to go down to the market with the farmer in his lorry. We used to leave at half four in the morning and take all the produce to Commercial Road in Portsmouth; that's where the whole area of farmers used to meet to sell their produce. You had to be down in the market by six. He only had an old Dennis lorry, he'd drop off to the local shops on the way down, in Havant, and get down in the market for the shopkeepers to buy their stuff before opening at nine.

Lawrence Shepherd, born 1927

Super Stewardess

My grandfather, his work was at Hayling Golf Club. The stewardess left and they had nobody to cook there, my grandmother stood in; she was the stewardess until she was forced to resign at the age of seventy-four! She didn't want to. She'd had a good run. I mean, they could have as many as a hundred on a match day. She did all the running of the bar and was responsible for the cleaning!

Mrs Janet Bocking, born 1939

On Mr Hedger's Farm

When I started, Hedger had the farm back this way. There was a lot of farmers, you see. Northwood Farm was A.H. Brown, and then we had Copper's, which was another, Banks'. I started for Mr Hedger when I left school.

There were only myself, the father and the two sons of Hedger's and there was four employees, but when I left there I went to Brown's, and I think there was about thirty of us; thirty to thirty-five at least. It was horses and small tractors then. Mainly was horse work when I first started. The tractors came in later. Used to be the old iron-wheeled tractors. Hedger's had one iron Ford and three horses. The tractors turned into it and the combine harvesters came into it a lot later. We had reapers, binders towed by the horses and then had to convert it with a different bar on to the tractor so the tractor could tow it.

We made the corn into sheaves and stand them up and carry 'em with the horse and wagon, put it in the rick and then wait for the local farmer from South Island who had a threshing-drum to come round and thresh the ricks out for them. He'd go to each farm when he was ready, give them a time when he could do it. He'd got his own threshing team.

John Plimbley and his future wife Ivy are among these young people on a Ham Farm milk lorry.

Workers at Ham Farm, South Hayling, having a well-earned rest from rick-building.

Hayling farm workers using conveyor belts to build a rick.

And then the workers on the farm jumped in and did what they had to do, and carted the corn away. His own threshing crew was feeder and bagger of the corn, and made sure all that was run on the lease way. They knew how the machine worked. They worked on his farm all the time, the crew he brought; but they did the threshing, the hoeing, milking – everything. It was all labour then.

Hedger's was general market gardening, lettuce, carrots, swedes, parsnips, sprouts; everything in the vegetable line.

He had a half a dozen or so cows – they all had a few cows – pigs, chickens, geese, that was up in the farmyard. There was always the farmer's wife looked after the animals and that was her pin-money, she called it, for her eggs and she killed a rooster for Christmas.

Lawrence Shepherd, born 1927

A Working Mum

I always went out to work, I used to clean houses, and I worked in Eastoke Corner post office, years ago, and then I went back into hairdressing again in Mengham. My mother was a nurse before she married, but never went out to work after. There is a difference there.

I went out to work when the two eldest were at school, I used to take the little one with me, have a bike seat and take her about. I went to work when the children were very small as well, 'cos a friend of mine used to look after my three, I'd do a stint and then I'd go and pick up her three and bring six of them back to lunch. We were both naval wives, in the same boat.

Mrs Patricia Gordon, born 1943

Silicon Valley or Hayling Island?

I worked fifteen years at Plessey's, West Leigh, which is how I came this way. We moved into Richmond Drive in 1961.

I joined the Plessey company when it took over the premises of a former Royal Naval design and research place [UDE, West Leigh]. We started developing a microprocessor. Plessey's were prepared to put in £4 million but it needed more money. As this was obviously goin' to be such a wonderful money-spinner for the nation, Plessey approached the government to match his £4 million. Harold Wilson said, 'No!' so if it'd carried on, we would have owned the world market, honestly we would have done – we'd gathered engineers from all over, with the particular expertise and suddenly this very specialist unit wasn't going to go anywhere.

I was offered about five or six jobs in the USA, suddenly we all had a jolly in the Strand Hotel, free meal, night out and all that – 'Sign here,' and they'd ship you and your family out and all, to a place that became known as Silicon Valley in California. I didn't want to go. We lived on Hayling Island by then.

F.T. Skipper, born 1932

Skipper Starts Up

Anyway, out of the blue I was offered a job with a Yankee computer company in Chichester, an offshoot from Control Data in IBM. I stayed with them two years, was Production Manager of the lot. The Americans set the place up but expected the British board to raise finance for the future. I wrote the plan they wanted for expansion into the British market, but they expected

British money to be on tap immediately, about £1.5 million. It was my job to raise the cash, but this all takes time, y'see?

I was getting moaned at from all quarters, so I left. I came home one night, said to my little wife – brave girl, you've got to have a brave wife! – 'I've had enough o' that. I've made fortunes for big companies all my working life, I think it's time I tried to make my own fortune!' She said, 'Well, do it! Don't talk about it, do it!' So we sold our house and I started up. We rented, and used the house money to start a Hayling factory.

F.T. Skipper, born 1932

Market Gardeners and Florists

I worked for my father. He wanted me to follow in his footsteps; mind you, I had the rough end of the stick. Others got time off, but he said, 'No, you've got to work like mad, you can't have half days.' It was a case of having to accept it, really. Just after the war there wasn't much else.

My father gardened for the love of gardening, whereas I did things for money. His idea was it didn't matter what you grew, it was bound to pay because you grew it yourself. 'But if you sell twenty-five items and throw seventy-five away,' I said, 'it's a waste of pots, time and the growing.' Gradually I got my own way.

Originally it was mostly vegetables. Tomatoes was one of my big things. Had quite a few greenhouses devoted to that, and then occasionally people would die and you'd get funerals. You'd make up a funeral with flowers. I thought, 'Holy Smoke! In a funeral you'd make – in a day's work – more money here than, well, the outside crops,

like peas and cabbage and that. There's a lot more money in funerals.'

Weddings were quite good, actually, and gradually the flower trade increased; the landscaping side I had to let go. We'd get everything ready to seed and they'd remind you from the shop that there was a funeral starting. It was frustrating. You'd be ploughing one minute, and then make up buttonholes. It's a good thing I'm a Gemini! Gradually the job changed me, really; I could see where the money lay. I was never happier than picking Brussels sprouts. But in floristry, in the end, people would say, 'This is a wonderful job,' and you know, for someone who didn't really excel at school this was quite something!

Peter Tibble, born 1932

Dress Shop and Miniskirt

I worked at Kitter's dress shop and we used to have the water come under the door, all in with the dresses and all up Creek Road. Creek Road now is all fruit machines. It spoils it. It used to be a café, gift shops. Holiday-makers came to look for gifts, especially those three little ducks on the wall – we used to sell boxes of those, and sticks of rock. The dress shop did very good business. I never got round to wearing miniskirts 'cos I never had the legs on me. My daughter did, she used to like wearing them.

Mrs Lilian Townsend-Holmes, born 1930

Novel Solutions

I'd find a problem somebody had and develop a novel solution: in the newspaper business, for measuring the dampness in newsprint (the ink will only take properly if the paper's at the right moisture content). I made little devices that would sense bearing temperature in weaving mills; the last thing they could have is the machine breaking down, so they had sensors all over the place. We designed them in our new Hayling factory. If I needed a specialist I would buy what was available.

As time went on, companies began getting their own expertise. I had a few very clever engineers; but that business was going, you had to spend a fortune in development. Then one day, I'd done something for a company and they said, 'Oh, could you make 500?' It was quite a challenge. All of a sudden it was, 'That was great, Skip – any chance of a thousand a month?' So I had to start a special unit to do that, and so it went on. Fortunately I didn't have to do any selling – we were only a tiny company and because, we were so good we could pick and choose work, y'know? So I expanded fairly quickly; my brother joined me in about 1976.

F.T. Skipper, born 1932

The Advent of Machines

Jan was company secretary, so I wasn't too involved with all the commercial stuff, that was alien. I tended to drop out, and my brother took over. At the most, we employed about 100 people.

We employed home-based workers on piece-work. Before I had a machine to 'ident'

A recruitment drive for Skipper Electronics, with Fred Skipper on the far left of the back row.

the wire, mums at home, they got ever so good. Many of the girls were married to men who could be sent abroad, for instance from IBM Havant. So the wives would go too. We adapted to using a changing staff of mostly women.

We were growing from day one; we spent twenty years looking for people, really. But then, as the industry got on, machines became available. I had two or three automatic soldering machines, which suddenly meant you didn't need four or five rows of girls soldering PC boards, not that we fired 'em, they just saved us having to employ more, and the same with some of the looming machines, used to clamp wires in the shape you set out as a template.

The wires are run in, according to where they have to go from and to, then bound together so that they can be all fixed into another device, for example a car, plane or television, all at once and connected up quickly [wiring looms were superseded in some cases by printed circuit boards]. To produce, say, 20,000, machines would be used, but smaller numbers, say 500, were wired by girls. A lot of prototype work was done by girls. You have to have a very skilled girl to make one, you know, the job was adapted as required.

The machines were destroying jobs. We just did not replace people. For instance, when we bought our first crimping machine, for putting terminations on the end of wires, we had rows and rows of them; rows of girls used to crimp by hand with special pliers. Very laborious. Then we acquired a machine that crimped 2,000 an hour. In the end, we had rows of these. So suddenly, apart from the prototype ladies, there was no hand-crimping at all.

F.T. Skipper, born 1932

Packets of Banknotes

The bank was Barclays Bank on Bank Corner, West Town. I went there as a junior clerk; there was only myself and the manager.

Because of bank rules, you weren't allowed to leave the building with one person in it, so you could only eat your lunch in the manager's room with your feet up on the table.

The bank used to pack old banknotes in brown paper packages labelled HVP (High Value Package); they were sent by registered letter to London so they would be destroyed and new ones issued. It was not supposed to be safe for one person to cycle down to the post office, along the road between Beachlands and the ferry.

The manager would wait until somebody responsible would come into the bank, like the local vicar, and say would he mind cycling down with his clerk to the post office? I mean think of that nowadays! We had an alarm bell after a time. We used to test it once a month. It would ring for five or ten minutes and eventually a girl would come in from next door and say, 'Do you know your bell's ringing?' Security wasn't absolutely marvellous!

We worked with cash on the till, same as now. You had to enter all the cheques up by hand into ledgers and into people's statements. The post was done in the same way, the post book in longhand. The first Biros were banned in the bank; they looked like carboned signatures, danger of fraud, you had to have permanent ink. A small heated piece of metal was used to seal letters. Rationing still on, bread units, everything was in short supply.

A.A.F. Bell, born 1927

Bath House and Beach Hut

The Bath House, many years ago, was where the people went in to change. When I worked there, it was a restaurant and shop, and we hired out bathing-costumes and towels and people used to come and eat there. I worked as a waitress. We served the usual tea and cakes. I don't think we had a changing place. And they did all the summer parties, you see. Apart from the Bath House was a big shed on the beach, by the beach huts. I did the parties in the shed when they had a busy season and the restaurant was full. Coach parties, like. And, when we weren't busy, sometimes I helped in the shop. It was quite nice, seeing all the people.

I did very well with my beach hut because casually somebody mentioned they had some children and I said, 'Well, the first beach hut is mine, if you'd like to use that?' and from then on I had people come, mostly nearly all the season. There was a Primus stove and everything you needed. Two chaps, they used to collect the key, then if they went home early, pop it through my letter-box at Pound Cottage.

Mrs Queenie Gates, born 1903

Brickyard Inventions

Father had worked in his father's brickyard, the time 1919; he worked there for fifteen years. My grandfather started making bricks after failing in market gardening. The ground was boggy; it was clay-bearing land and he started a brickyard. In 1910 or 1911. Father, he used the same method, slip-moulds, but he didn't tread the clay by bare feet. He made a pug-mill to grind the clay and he used a Ruston Hornsby engine; he made the machine out of a roller; mangles from the

South Hayling Beach with the Bath House on the left, and bathing machines near the water.

Brickmaking gang, 1935. Standing, left to right: Geoff White, Bert Smith, Frank Siville (?), Harold Pycroft, with Fred Griffiths on the ladder.

Noel Pycroft setting bricks on a hack, c. 1948.

laundry, made that out of wood – the cogs – and engine. He made it out of wood and boards, and made the blades out of a drop-keel of a boat; he went to the blacksmith's, of a night, and cut and shaped a square end for it. About 1934. He only had a oil engine for about a twelvemonth and then he went for electric.

Noel Pycroft, born 1928

Fishing on Hayling

Virtually all the commercial fishermen lived on Hayling, a lot more than now. There's probably only a handful, from Hayling, left. If you moored in Chichester or Langstone harbours, you would've been either from Chichester, Hayling or Portsmouth, on the swinging moorings down at Langstone. Now, they're all mainly using marinas; I mean, they're expensive but you step straight on and off your boat, there's no trying to row out against the tides. I used Northney Marina quite a bit; Sparkes' Marina and Langstone Marina over on Eastney as well are used by fishermen.

Oyster catching still goes on, in the harbours, which are an open ground still, between November and April. In the old days, 1970s and '80s, you started at midnight. There'd be 90 or 100 vessels; they started on the clock, which was good fun. Nowadays it starts eight o'clock in the morning – you might only get fifteen to twenty boats up there.

Fishermen are getting the same sort of prices now as they were twenty years ago, so it's not such a good earner as it used to be.

Fishing, we started off with gill-nets, very like tangle-nets. They are on the sea bed, you've got an anchor either end and you go up and down the tide, so you're not catching as much weed as if you went across the tide. They are rigged with very light netting, so when a fish touches it, it will tangle its way up into the net itself and be trapped until you haul the nets the following day. So we lay them down at night and pick them up very, very early light: take the fish out once it's on board, clean through the nets, re-lay them and set them, then lay them back out the following night again.

Ian Griffiths, born 1964

The Fishing Year

In the year, you're oystering from November to April, your plaice starts to run around the April time, into tangle-nets, or you're trawling or potting – there's an awful lot of potting round here for crabs, lobsters and whelks. About March, April time, your cuttlefish start running. You see the bones washed up on the beach? It's like a massive squid, they come in to spawn and when they spawn they die off. That's why you see the bone after. You'll see a lot of vessels going up and down the sea front that time of year; that's what they're catching. After that, they go back on the wet fish side, or the potting side, until November comes again and start the oyster season up.

I stopped fishing. I love fishing – but I bought Seddon's, as it was before I changed the name to the Solent Fish Company, and trying to fish and run the shop, I just wasn't dedicating enough time to fishing. You've got to be out there for hours, concentrate, study what's happening with the patterns where the

fish are going. So I sold my vessel – it went to Alderney – and concentrated on the shop, built the business up from there. I bought the shop February 1992, and the boat must have gone about 1993 or '94. We're a very busy little company. We supply naval bases, colleges, butchers, caterers and restaurants.

Ian Griffiths, born 1964

The Lifeboat Tradition

I'm president of Mengham Rythe Sailing Club and chairman of the lifeboat station as well, having been in that since its inception in 1975. The second station started in 1975. The first one disbanded when Selsey and Bembridge lifeboats had engines put in; 1924 I think. They didn't need to row off, you see.

I understand from relatives of the coxswain that they were terribly distressed when Hayling lost its lifeboat. It was in 1974 that they reconstituted the station, at the entrance to Chichester Harbour. An Atlantic class lifeboat, it was then; and I've been involved ever since. We had two of the old lifeboatmen who were still alive at the opening in 1974, so it's got a continuance; well, one was Steve Goldring and one was Cecil Bonniface. I was presented with a Keith Shackleton painting when I retired from the secretaryship of the local branch of the Royal National Lifeboat Institution, subscribed to by all the Islanders and crews.

Roy Smith, born 1923

Lifeboat Rescues

Two big rescues Rod James and Graham Raines did on the bank, just outside the

The volunteers of the Hayling Island lifeboat crew, 1920. Steve Goldring is on the far left of the middle row.

harbour. One was a boy on the sea-wall, Rod James – he's just retired, school teacher – got him; he was playing, dodging the waves, and a wave caught him and took him in the sea. That was a very rough day, force nine south-easterly gale. The boy hung on to a breakwater, about 20 yards out. The lifeboat couldn't reach him, so Rod swam to him and he disappeared so Rod had to wait for him to come up. He took him ashore where other lads from the lifeboat were standing by to drag him over the wall. They were both bruised and battered but for that he was awarded a silver medal in 1981.

The other silver medal was awarded when a yacht capsized on the bar. Two people were thrown in the water, the lifeboat was called. This chap was at the end of his tether and sinking, but Graham Raines held him up. The returning lifeboat went right over them both in the very rough sea, but the coxswain realized this, stopped the propellers and both men came up at the back of the boat, the rescued man still unconscious. Rod James was also in that boat, went to help him back in and was tipped out into the water. And no way they could get back on board themselves. One of the Portsmouth lifeboat crew, called to help, leapt aboard the Hayling boat, and helped them out, in turn got the casualty out. There's only three, you see, on the Atlantic class lifeboat.

Roy Smith, born 1923

HAYLING ISLAND SAILING CLUB
75th ANNIVERSARY CELEBRATIONS

Come and Join our

PARADE OF SAIL
Sunday 30th June 1996

To celebrate HISC's 75 years of sailing, we are organising a PARADE OF SAIL.

Do you own a Classic Boat, or a Class Boat with an early number?

We hope all old boats still sailing in the harbour will attend and expect most types of dinghy to be represented

Programme		How to enter
10 – 11.00	Registration	Please contact HISC for entry form
11.30	Parade of Boats	to be returned by 1st June if possible.
13.00	Ashore for refreshments	tel. 01705 463768

High Tide – 11.20

A Parade of Sail celebrates 75 years of the Hayling Island Sailing Club.

CHAPTER 10

Leisure

A Congregational church garden party at Dr Broughton's.

Open Gardens for the Lifeboats

The centenary year of the Horticultural Society was 1986. We displayed our own gardens to people, in our case about the middle of July. It was a late season, we were having trouble getting the flowers out in time to make anything of a show. You can't alter the weather, can you? The flowers were out but the rambler roses, which are always out in July, weren't on this occasion. The vine was there in full leaf.

We each chose which weekend we thought the garden was at its best and everybody came to look at each other's gardens, but others came as well, it was a public thing. I think there were six or eight of the gardens, or maybe more, open to the public. And we raised money for the RNLI, which came in the end to £2,676 which was very good, donated by people who came to look at the gardens.

Mrs Margaret Hitchcock, born 1923

Apprenctices' Outing

I belonged to the Cyclists' Touring Club and, with friends, would come to Hayling by ferry, with bicycles and sandwiches, during the war; and later by bus, with my family.

Hayling had very fine, white sand. On returning from the Army in 1948, I became foreman of a small workshop for electrical engineers. My first wife and I used to take the apprentices to Hayling for Sunday outings.

J.E. Baxter, born 1927

Church and Social Life

I was confirmed at Hayling, but I always went to chapel as a girl. I still have the Bible my chapel gave me when I left to go into service. I go to church every week now, because I can please myself, but I always supported church events. I belonged to the Townswomen's Guild and I used to be in the drama group. We lived in North Hayling thirty years before we had a car; it was a real treat.

Mrs Eva Prior, born 1910

The Excitement of Ocean Racing

My sailing grew more and more exciting as I became more and more qualified, and ending up with ocean racing, because a very well-known gentleman, Capt. John Illingworth, lived at Fleet Manor – my

'Ancient Britons', a scene from Hayling's 1949 pageant held at Mengham Farm.

Mesdames Curtis (Wall), Hollinshead (Queen) and Tucker are among the cast in this scene from the 1949 pageant.

father had actually sold him the house – and I was introduced because I was interested in sailing and in no time at all I was doing trials with him. He was a designer, and I used to go out in the yachts with them while they all hoisted the sails, and he said, 'You must come ocean racing, with us!' Well, you wonder why you are going! Everybody who goes ocean racing says to themselves, 'Why are we out here?' But it is the most wonderful experience. He very kindly made me a member of the Royal Ocean Racing Club – it opened great doors to me.

Beryl, Lady Mackworth, born 1915

Teenage Days

Tuesdays was Scouts, Thursday evening was homework, Saturday mornings I worked, but Saturday afternoons in winter was football,

then we used to all go to pictures in the evening. And I used to do a milk round Sunday mornings from about 6.00 a.m. onwards to get a half-crown so I'd got enough money in my pocket to spend, when I was about sixteen.

Colin Vaughn, born 1932

Dancing at the Nab Club

I moved to Hayling aged sixteen. I used to go to the Nab Club, a night-club – very different from what they have today – oh, just a nice and ordinary little club. No drugs, not even much drinking. You used to meet the boys and have a dance and I used to walk home to Rails Lane, often on my own, skipping along the beach in the moonlight. I mean, you wouldn't now, would you? I wouldn't. We used to go to dances in Southsea, in a coach. The Hayling

Audrey Tyrrell and friends dressed for a dance, c. 1956.

buses didn't run late, I'd have had to leave about 9.00 p.m. to go home by bus.

Mrs Audrey Cozens (née Tyrrell), born 1939

Church Activities

Our family belonged to the Free church [now the Baptist church]. They joined in a lot of church activities.

Three times a Sunday we used to go to church. I won certificates for scripture – we used to go to the Misses Marsh's. Oh, they were an old interesting family, the Marshes and the Darleys; the Darleys had Queensbury Lodge, the end of Hollow Lane. And we used to go to Portsmouth to the Wesleyan church to pick up these certificates – all framed beautifully, and books we used to win as prizes. But I can't say I'm religious now.

Mrs Grace Townsend, born 1924

The Amateur Dramatic Society

Friends of friends said, 'Come down and join,' and that was thirty years ago – I got involved as an actor, general odds-bod, in the Barn Theatre. Then I not exactly left the society [Hayling Island Amateur Dramatic Society], but I had other things to do so I couldn't get involved at different times. About twelve years ago, I got more involved again, more on the producing side than acting. I enjoy artistic work, did a lot of their set designs.

Eric Dossetter, born 1942

Friendly Competition

The Dramatic Society [HIADS] was at the Barn Theatre slightly before me. We were great friends, sort of rivals because I was a professional school, for which people paid me, whereas they were amateur. And we got on terribly well. I did supply the dancers for the pantomimes but I'm afraid it was ballet training that I trained the girls of Hayling. But the Barn Theatre was a great success.

Beryl, Lady Mackworth, born 1915

A Centenary Show

At that time, 1996, we had one show a year. One of our members grew all these vegetables that they grew in 1886, the old-fashioned celery, and striped beans. He made a point of getting the seed that was current in the 1880s – all those were grown especially for the show, the old-fashioned varieties. Tomatoes, were they striped or something? I thought they were very odd. Beans, all sorts of beans. The parsnips aren't as big as the modern parsnips; I mean that's how they were at the time.

Mrs Margaret Hitchcock, born 1923

Organizations and Activities

One of the things I like about Hayling is that you meet some of the same people in lots of different situations and organizations,

so it's quite easy to make friends. I've been most to the Mengham Women's Institute, which, like all WIs, has lots of subsections, and you get to know the people in your particular one. I joined a Readers' Group, we just read poems or books which are on a theme and we have a lot of fun, and a cup of tea at the end of it, in Daisy's house.

We've been to quite a lot of the productions at the Station Theatre. We've really enjoyed that. We also joined the local Bosmere Hundred Society, which is a kind of historical society, connected with the environment and so on, and it's a good social centre as well.

The Community Hall has a church, adult education, horticultural shows, a youth club, various other clubs, an occasional blood-donor session, the polling station, and

Hayling Townswomen's Guild choir, 1952.

The show committee at the centenary of Hayling Island Horticultural Society.

Bill Scarratt and Avril Miller at a Horticultural Society summer show during the 1980s.

much more. We went to a folk dance – they got about 150 people there, in aid of the British Heart Foundation, and they're going to have another one next year. People had come from Petersfield, Waterlooville, Cowplain, as well as local people. So it just goes to show that Hayling's not nearly so isolated as it used to be.

Patricia Ross, born 1929

Community Spirit

Certain residents got together, several of whom are still connected with the centre here. Ken Aires, who is going to be our new president, was one of the founders, there's several still around, and our volunteers – that man the reception desk – a lot of those have been there since it was built.

There's a lot of adult education. Drawing and painting has always been very successful, silk painting was popular and dressmaking. Whether it's because the adult education fees have gone up so much – they really struggle to get the numbers at the beginning. We have aerobics, which they call aerobic dancing, but, I mean, I've done it and it doesn't seem like dancing to me! We have modern sequence dancing, not a class, it's just a club, but they always need more people. Some of them are in their eighties, it's amazing, in fact it's probably the older age groups that like that sort of dancing, can't imagine the youngsters, can you? We've had badminton and keep fit, ladies' keep fit, and Dawn Jacobs does the body maintenance and callisthenics. There's yoga, Mrs Fine runs that, ju-jitsu. American line dancing we have; it's very popular.

For the little ones, we have parents and

The choir of Mengham Women's Institute takes part in a county choir festival at Littlehampton.

Mengham WI on a day trip to Bruges via the Channel Tunnel.

toddlers groups – we're heaving on a Thursday morning. That's been going on for years and years – and Toyland Library, they can come and borrow for a minimal sum everything from a child's video to a little car. We are negotiating for Hayling Youth Project to have a youth club back here, because it's the one age group you'll find most community centres are not catered for. There's the Canine Partners for Independence, their Bonio award-winning dog is Ensor; we've got a quiz night soon and at least one of the dogs will be appearing – if not answering questions!

Elyane Jones, born 1944

Scouting Life

I started Scouting when I was eight, that was 1940, that was where the headquarters are now, King's Road, but there was just a muddy track up to the HQ. We used to try and keep our shoes clean ready for inspection. I suppose I'm still Scouting now, really. I enjoy my Scouting very much. I felt that I should give back something to the people that took us during the war, really, when there wasn't a lot that we could do.

When I was about eighteen I got my Queen's Scout award and then went on to be an Assistant Scout Leader, 1950ish, with the Hayling troop. Jack Derben was the leader. Gran Derben was the cook in the golf course. Jack next door came out of the Army about 1946-1947 and took over the Scout troop. Then when he retired, his son John took over as Group Scoutmaster and I took over. We had a reasonable-sized Scout troop, about thirty boys.

We had one Scout troop and one Cub

Hayling Scout leaders, 1946. From left to right: F. Barrett, Jack Derben, ? Foster, G. Steele, P. Tilney, E. Durrel, and ? Pinkney.

Scout camp at Luccombe, Somerset, c. 1947. Standing at the back are, from left to right: J. Muggridge, Ted Watson, Harry Spooner, Henry Durrel, M. Sprinks, J. Muxworthy, Scoutmaster Jack Derben, Glyn Bradley, D. Cole, G. Grant, R. Hill, Queen's Scout Colin Vaughn, and Ken Doble.

pack – John then made it up to about five Cub packs. The troop built up to fifty, and I couldn't cope with that number of boys in the troop, so we split it in half, one on a Tuesday and one on a Thursday; when the Island grew.

Then when John went on to become District Commissioner, I became Group Scoutmaster of the 3rd Hayling Scout Group for sixteen to seventeen years. I was awarded the Silver Wolf award from the Chief Scout about 1959, for services to Scouting. I retired at sixty. I did forty-odd years as a uniformed leader. I've been in Scouting for nigh on sixty years. I'm still working as an executive committee member in Havant area. I grow orchids as a hobby, have for about thirty years.

Colin Vaughn, born 1932

Fundraising Together

I joined the fund-raisers for the RNLI first in 1970, was elected Deputy Launching Officer of the lifeboat station for two years, and I enjoyed it; Honorary Secretary for twelve years and when I retired I thought, 'Well, it's time for a younger man to take on.'

I became chairman of the station committee – I'm now president – and was awarded a Gold Badge in 1998 for services to the Lifeboat Service.

With my wife, one year, we raised £1,079, which we thought was remarkable from knocking on doors, just on the Island. We did that work together.

Roy Smith, born 1923

Members of the Hayling Island lifeboat crew at an open day, 1999. The volunteers of the Hayling crew were called out 80 times in the past year. The two lifeboats are an Atlantic class boat Betty Battle *and a 'D' class boat* Leonard Steadman.

CHAPTER 11

Wartime Memories

Servicemen on the step of the Nab Club.

Troops on Hayling

In 1939 the only thing was, the troops being brought onto the Island, which was something which we'd never had before, naturally. I lived at North Hayling, quite near the holiday camp, and they were self-contained there. We used to have the flat-bottomed boats going up to the bridge and back again; there was the gun-site at North Hayling of course and the gun-site at Sinah.

I suppose I had a trousseau, and had enough to be going on with but I can't think that I had any problems with clothing coupons. Food? I mean, you've got sausages and you've got mince, I think you just sort of made your own day to day meals as you went along really. Having our own eggs helped. I suppose we got shortages of this and that but then you subsidized it with something else. Can't say that we ever went hungry. In Northney, naval personnel were the only strangers we saw.

Mrs Joyce Poore (née Nichol), born 1919

Sea Defences

I was fifteen, sixteen when the war began. I was scared because they started building the sea defences. We weren't allowed on the beach.

Mrs Grace Townsend, born 1924

A Schoolboy's War

I did lose a very good friend of mine, really. I used to walk up from the council houses towards the Manor Farm. On the left-hand side there was some houses, cottages, and my school-friend used to live there. I used to always to pick him up on the way up to school. And this particular morning, when I went there, there was a policeman: I said, 'Where's Bert?' He says, 'Oh, you carry on up to school, he'll come along later' but I didn't realize the air-raid shelter had had more or less a direct hit and he was killed.

I remember coming home from school one dinner time, 'cos you used to run home to dinner and go back again, and the German was machine-gunning all across the fields and we were running along Manor Road and we jumped in the ditch. I remember that quite well really. But other than that, the war didn't affect me much. Not as children, you still went to school and you just went to the air-raid shelter every evening or you probably slept in the shelter, just down the bottom of the garden.

I've got a piece of land-mine cord that came from the land-mine that dropped in West Town. My aunt lived in West Town next to – I still call it King's the paper shop, it was a one-stop shop – and the land-mine dropped opposite the chemist's, right in the middle of the road. I remember walking round there and looking at the hole in the ground, and the policeman said, 'Here's a piece of parachute cord you can have' which I still have – a memento, I suppose.

Colin Vaughn, born 1932

Colin Vaughn with parachute cord from the West Town land-mine.

The old Congregational church which was destroyed by a land-mine in 1942.

Bombed Out

Our church was bombed down the night that we were bombed out. I was seventeen. We went to live with relatives for six months then we came back to South Road. The Cleeves owned the house then, they owned a lot of the land round here.

Mrs Grace Townsend, born 1924

Explosive Syrup Tin

When they dropped bombs here, we used to hunt for this explosive, which was like a lump of beeswax, burn it and see if it would explode. What we done, we got a small Ovaltine tin and filled it, put the lid on that; we got a Tate & Lyle's golden syrup tin, soldered the lid on that, wi' silver solder; then threw it on the fire,

and I remember my cousin put his head round and said, 'Has it gone off?' and 'Bang!' the tin collapsed and stuck like a big knife in the tree right at the side of his head.

Aircraft crashed and we got bullets. We used to hit them on concrete posts. The Very bullets, they had colours, you see, and one went out through Mr Voake's caravan. We blew the post to pieces. And he complained that we was dangerous. I suppose it was dangerous. I got the cane for that at school, you got punished at school for everything, when you were in mischief.

Noel Pycroft, born 1928

Finding Shelter

I vividly remember the doodle-bugs. The air-raid shelter, an Anderson, it was actually buried in the ground. It had a bit of water in the bottom. First of all, we used to go under the stairs, then we went under a big table in the corner in the lounge, then we ended up in a shelter in the back of the garden. Mother was an air-raid warden, so there was a lot of to-ing and fro-ing with Mother – and Dad was in the Army, Royal Engineers.

John Derben OBE, born 1937

Beyond the Bombs

Mother was a nurse, always helping her ageing family. One awful night, Grandmother's father died: Mr Bastable of Rose Cottage, South Road. My mother went down to lay him out and they left him in the bedroom. The bombing started. My mother ran back up to Church Road, as fast as she could, to us and my grandmother. That night, Rose Cottage was bombed and he was buried in the rubble but he had already died and they had to find him in the rubble to bury him again in the churchyard!

Mrs Janet Bocking, born 1939

Building Bombers

I started to drink at the Royal Oak when I worked at the factory. We were making the gliders, and parts for the Airspeed Oxford. We didn't know where they were assembled. We knew what we were working on. It was good work, ruined my hands though. Planes were made of wood. That's where I met my second husband. He was a cabinet-maker. It was beautiful work, they were all sandpapered. We used to make these gussets. It was really interesting. Then De

Havilland's came into it; I made the bombers' chest ramps for Mosquitoes. We used to do fire-watch and we had the doodle-bugs come over.

Mrs Grace Townsend, born 1924

Stuck in a Shelter

Of course, they did make the Mulberry Harbours – that was all secret, it was all heavily guarded, but, as kids, we used to clamber in amongst the wire and you'd hardly be an enemy soldier, that size and in short trousers!

To direct the Blitz from Portsmouth, they lit beacon fires, you see, once you lit the fires the enemy thought, 'This is it' and they unloaded all their bombs. There were twenty-four incendiaries and a land-mine on our nursery. I mean, they thought they was hitting a strategic target. There was lots of sailors and soldiers out there doing jobs and you'd hear them shouting up the street, which was a bit comforting if you were stuck in the shelter. It was horrible being, like, in a tin box. When our land-mine went off, we were just a short distance away. The light blew out, you see. I was scared, really, when that happened, 'cos its just a small tin and I think I'd sooner have b'n out, you know, you felt like getting out of it.

Peter Tibble, born 1932

Pigs and Swill

Oh, yes, we had rationing – we kept a pig which we had a half of. Course, we got swill from the shipyard where, well, half a dozen girls from Hayling worked in the canteen there. There were lots of, see, yacht havens, down on Copse Lane.

Noel Pycroft, born 1928

The Bakery is Bombed

Investment Insurance uses a shop I built on the site of a bakery, bombed at the beginning of the war. I bought it as a derelict site. The bakery was underground and the whole house above fell into the hole. The baker was a Mr Biggs, and he moved to Mengham.

D. Collins, born 1917

Cycling for Shrapnel

We just used to hear where the bomb had come down and cycle down and look into the bomb holes, really. We used to find shell caps and bits of old rocket and so on. I used to collect them at one time, then lost interest. We were about the only house in West Town which was not seriously damaged by bombs, because we had a band of trees between us and a land-mine.

Michael Camp, born 1933

Troops at the Nab Club

I remember the bombing of Portsmouth; it was a shocking sight, night after night, and the fights in the sky when the planes were being chased. We were so lucky on the Island. One German plane did come down at Sandy Point [in the Creek Road area]; the pilot was brought to the Nab Club and the police came and took him away.

My parents were not in the services, my two brothers were in the RAF and I was an air-raid warden. Our guest-house only had two seasons before war broke out; we lived there all through the war; we continued to run the Nab Club, as there were lots of troops stationed all round Eastoke and Sandy Point. They belonged to the Royal Marines, the Royal Navy, the Army and there were French Canadians. They lived under canvas or in holiday camps. We made friends with all of them and they were kind and helpful to mother and myself.

Mrs Mary Voller (née Tickner), born 1923

Looking After the Boat-Yard

It was quite amazing because both my brothers and my sister were in the RAF and with a large family, during the war, if there was an elderly parent, they'd usually release the last member of the family without calling up; but I was also exempt because of the boat-yard. The Navy took it over. My first husband went into the Solent Patrol, at sea when war was declared, in an armed yacht – and I was left and went down to my parents and these houses were all requisitioned, on Sandy Point Estate. But I had to look after the boat-yard.

I saw the biggest raid on Thorney Island. My brother was home, he was a survivor from the Glorious. We watched from the Sailing Club. Those hangers you could see going up into the air, and these Junkers 88s came in. The incredible thing was, in no time at all our fighters from Tangmere were here and there were lots of casualties coming down in the mud, but the Navy came and rescued them.

Beryl, Lady Mackworth, born 1915

Rosemary Nichol in the garden at Northney, 1951.

Baby's Gas Mask

When my daughter Rosemary was born I used to take her in the pram with the blessed thing stuck underneath – you know, the infant's gas mask which you could put a baby right into. I was away for two years during the war with my husband, who was an Army instructor. On the Island, what used to worry us more than anything was when the guns went off at the gun-site. You were just going to drink a cup of tea or something and …!!

When our daughter Rosemary was about six months and my friend's daughter three months, we went to a tiny beach, the one Sunday afternoon that Thorney Island was bombed, and that was quite an experience. The bombs were just coming down all the time. Alan wasn't born until six years later.

Mrs Joyce Poore (née Nichol), born 1919

Building Beach Defences

They made these blocks on the beach. Just made a box, filled it up wi' concrete, took the shuttering away, next made another box – there! But they were doing it in sequence all along the beach, not very far apart, you could, I dunno, you could ride your bike through 'em but you couldn't drive a car through them.

Noel Pycroft, born 1928

The Bath House Closes

All the beach huts were cleared off the beach, and I was very lucky because the last year I was working at the Bath House I sold my beach hut, so I didn't lose it. And the Bath House closed for the war, for the

Rosemary's little brother Alan at Northney.

invasion. They had all sorts of things on the beach, I never went down till after the war.

Mrs Queenie Gates, born 1903

Home During Wartime

I was born virtually as war broke out and my father went off to the war when I was still in a cot. He was in the Army, and my mother knew nobody in Reading, where we were lodging because his work was in Reading, and she came back to live in the house that my grandparents had built on the Island. She came to be near the rest of the family.

Mrs Janet Bocking, born 1939

Teaching in Portsmouth

I was teaching first of all – I wasn't married then – in Drayton Road School in Portsmouth. We had, you know, those great big barrage balloons actually in the playground. I taught at that school until it was bombed out.

Mrs Brenda Wood, born 1915

Bombed Out of Portsmouth

My family home in Portsmouth was destroyed by bombs as were the houses of my brothers, who were in business with my father. I lived with my grandmother at Hambledon but followed my husband round the country when I could. He was in the Army.

Mrs A., born 1920

The Meadowsweet Canteen

In the war, I must have been working casually for a bit, and I had my daughter. I was working at Hedger's Farm, for quite a while, because Jim, old Mr Hedger, was getting very frail. I used to see to him. Did the general housework and in between I used to go up and help Mrs Les Hedger in Clovelly Road. On the corner the Miss Rouses had the Meadowsweet Canteen, and we used to go evenings, voluntary, like, to do the cooking. When I was with Mrs Hedger in Clovelly Road, they used to make the trifles in the house. We'd knock up a bit of sponge-cakes of some sort, and then orangeade, and whip the custard and oh, they went down fine. The sailors loved them. And of course the farm was so good to the canteen. They would send up potatoes; if the peas were in, they used to come up for their dinners. We'd all set to and chuck the peas. We'd do meat balls, they ate up goodness knows what, the sailors. Then, the camp was good; any spare things. The camp was HMS Northney then.

Mrs Queenie Gates, born 1903

Visiting the Canteen

I used to go up to the canteen one night a week, Doris worked more often but of course I had Roger, the baby. But they used to cook them nice food. I always remember the spring cabbage, because it was always nice and crispy and they used to make nice sausages, you know, and of course we had bits of supper there and, I mean, we didn't get much in the food line in the war when we think back. They were lovely ladies who ran the canteen, and the men were all polite too, there was never any rudeness or taking advantage, you know? They, the Misses Rouse, didn't do the cooking, there used to be two or three local ladies up; I used to go with Mrs Hedger. I don't remember any of the Army girls but I had a Wren here because they wanted homes for Wrens off of the camp.

Mrs Eva Prior, born 1910

Cooking for Mountbatten

Northney Holiday Camp was HMS Northney then; it was the sailors. And there were sailors at the end of the garden, for the invasion, in a tent. Until the planes came over. The sailors built my air-raid shelter. Then there were the Marines. At night, I never saw them, mind, they had black faces, but they used to call out, 'Where's the cocoa, then?' and I'd make a jug of cocoa.

The bungalow opposite Clovelly Road, the Navy took that over, that was officers' quarters. Any captain that was in the camp, that was the captain's house. The first was Capt. Dawson; well, he went, then I had Capt. Chambers – I got handed over, you see. I used to go and cook there for whoever was visiting. The camp was all secret.

One we had to dinner quite a lot was Sir Roger Keyes. Oh, he was a lovely man! He wasn't very tall. So friendly.

I really shouldn't say who else came, it was all so secret. I never knew who was coming, I was told we'd have a dinner, we'd have visitors, and about half an hour or so before they come Mrs Chambers would say,

The boat party football team, 1943/44. For former Leading Seaman A. Sharples (front row, second from the right) this photograph is a souvenir of his time spent on Hayling Island during the Second World War.

'You'll never know who's coming today! We've got Louis Mountbatten coming' and he was a lovely man. Tall, and a voice! It boomed! And I remember I cooked in the kitchen and there was a little door there – we had a batman, Jim – he was another Hedger, but no relation to the farm, he used to squeeze through and take the meals through. They'd pass the dirty plates out to me. I could see them. He'd chat to me. Quite nice, quite nice.

I do remember I made Mountbatten, somebody must have given us apples, 'cos we were grateful for anything that got given us, you know, and I made him apple fritters. He said that was the best he'd ever tasted. He hadn't had apple fritters since he was a child! He came out and thanked me for the apple fritters. I don't know what he thought of the first course – I gave him a marrow souffle.

But they used to eat everything that was sent in. It was quite exciting, but I never knew. Sometimes I opened the door for them and I've offered them a sherry if the batman wasn't around.

Mrs Queenie Gates, born 1903

A Baby for HMS Northney

I was stationed at HMS Northney, and I was lucky to have my wife with me for fourteen to sixteen months, thanks to Floss Carter, who let us have a bed-sit at No. 18 Northney Road. When she knew that my wife, Jessie, was pregnant, Floss Carter insisted that the baby be born at our little bed-sit. The midwife was Nurse Curtis, a good friend to us. You can imagine the comments from personnel going into Havant, when I had to wheel a new pram from Havant to No. 18 Northney Road!

Mrs Queenie Gates cooked apple fritters for Lord Louis Mountbatten.

The late Mrs Gamblin, who lived near the Royal Oak, Langstone, bought us a christening robe for our daughter. She also gave us cockles in a jar, to eat on our way back home. We used to have a sing-song in the Oak. A rather stout lady played the piano. Her signature tune was 'Any Old Iron'.

Arnold Sharples
Former Leading Seaman

On Guard

As drivers with the 2nd Mobile Naval Base Defence Organization, those on the guard roster were instructed by a military training instructor to adopt an 'on guard' position, with the rifle at waist level and in a loud voice say,

The Royal Hotel on Hayling Seafront was the home of a school of musketry in the First World War, and was occupied by Combined Operations during the Second World War. The building has since been converted into flats.

'Halt, who goes there?' When satisfied, one would reply, 'Pass, friend'. When I stepped forward for my turn, I shouted, 'Halt, who goes there!' followed by an equally loud 'Please?' The other members of the guard doubled up, but the Corporal Marine training instructor told me that I was not checking guests at a garden party or words to that effect. I still think of those happy days at Hayling.

Jack Sinclair, born 1921
Former Royal Marine
stationed on Hayling 1941

Waiting for the Invasion

My brother was in the Army and I was at sea, so when the soldiers parked in the roads – we lived down near Eastoke – my father and mother were always making tea; they felt they would like to think that some of their own sons were being given tea or whatever, wherever they were.

But the whole of the Island was a no go zone, you couldn't get onto the Island by the D-Day. I didn't get home at all for a few weeks, but prior to the invasion we were all in the Solent waiting to go. We were anchored off Lee-on-Solent and there were so many ships! How the Germans didn't spot us I don't know.

The other thing that amazed me was round the back of Selsey Bill they took these big Mulberries, and sunk them – the big Mulberry units and all the bits. The Germans flying over must have wondered what that was, because there was all the tugs looking after them, and then a couple of days before, they took them all up and towed them across and the Germans never twigged it. Oh, making the Mulberries, on the French side of the Channel: first of all I was launchman, running about in the boat, trying to get people ashore because there was all these communications and things, and all we had, before they put the harbour down, got the thing built up on the beach-heads, was they sank an old French cruiser that we could just get alongside and tie up and give some shelter.

Roy Smith, born 1923

Golf Club Dances

When we first went to Hayling Island, the officers mess was at Westfield Oaks, there was a road which went on up out of the Island and it was just off to the right there, we had oak trees in the gardens.

We used to have dances at the golf club and I remember once, the dance was going very well and we had to stop at midnight or something and I altered the clock so we went on another hour! There was the Shades bar and I think officers kept out of that; and there was another pub up at Station Road.

Col. John d'E Coke RM, born 1916

The Germans are Coming!

People these days don't realize what exciting lives us youngsters had, but, do you know, I walked from Puffing Billy? Where the Station Theatre is? Well, it was the station – I walked from there one night – came back off leave and my friend Pat was s'posed to have met me and she said, 'If I'm not there, don't wait, because obviously I've been called out' because we never knew. So I said, 'Okay'. Well, when I arrived there, she wasn't there so I just cut through the woods at the side. You know Sinah Lane? And it was all woods behind Staunton Avenue, with paths, but no fear, no lights either!

And do you want to hear the next bit? When I got out of the other end, with my little case, out of the bushes jumped – a man! All black, a hat on and uniform. I jumped up and he went, 'Shh...shshsh! Don't make a noise, don't make a noise! We're attacking the camp!' And I thought, 'It's the Germans!' So I dropped my case, and I ran screaming up the road, 'The Germans are coming!' and sat down so he said, 'Shut up you silly Moo' – I'll use that word! He said, 'They're supposed to be attacking the camp as practice!' Well, would anybody walk through woods like, now? Not many people walk out on their own of a night.

Mrs Dot Watson (née Friend), born 1921
Former Corporal, Auxiliary Territorial Service

A Land Girl

I came to Hayling in 1938 from Bath with my family and at sixteen I joined the Women's Land Army. I worked at Mr Cleeve's farm. It's a caravan site now. I lived at home.

The job was strawberry picking, sprout picking, potato picking. I moved to Arbuthnot's, down at the ferry, that was a pig farm. And from there I went to Tournebury Farm as a milkmaid, that was Snell's [of Mengham House], it's now a golf course. And when he sold up I went to Mr

'The Gang', 1944: Hayling Land Army girls with Bill Brown (left), Mr D. Walters (right) and Dawn the dog. The land girls are, from left to right, back row: G. Smith, A. Short, W. Turner, P. Rowe, J. Parsons, E. Newland, J. Charman; front row: V. Wilkinson, P. Rowe, G. Smith, B. Wrixon.

Walters'. That's got houses built on it. Then I worked at the manor, for Mr Walters. I liked strawberry picking and haymaking but I was scared of cows!

When the war started, I enjoyed the dances at the servicemen's camps. The Royal Marines were at the Sunshine, and the Victoria Hall had dances every week. Hayling was full of servicemen. My father ran a second-hand shop and was too old to be called up.

Mrs Ivy Plimbley (née Wakely)

A Dreadful Raid

We didn't come and live here permanently until 1946. I was in London in the war, we were allowed to come down, but when the Marines requisitioned the bungalow, they put a family in there; one of my brother's bikes got messed up, they'd been riding it along in the salt water. But when we could, we used to come down to the bungalow. It was very heavily defended, you know, all concrete blocks and great big barbed wire stuff and everything. That friend that I told you about I lost last year, she found a dead German body, on the beach, and sticking out of the sand.

Oh, I was here when there was a very bad raid and they dropped a lot of land-mines; in fact it was the night the Tizzards, old Mrs Tizzard, was killed in Tournebury Lane. That was the butcher's mother. It was a dreadful raid. But I was only eight or nine.

Mrs Mavis Chamberlain (née Tucker),
1936-2000

CHAPTER 12

Changes

Staunton Avenue with fields on the right. (photograph: Hayling Library)

Delivery by Horse and Cart

I had nappies, terry and muslin ones. They didn't have all these Pampers and things like they do now. I mean, we had to wash them all. We had a coal fire. Hayling Coal and Transport, they used to import coal at the bridge, outside the Ship, there was always a barge coming. I think Hayling Coal and Transport always delivered by horse and cart; so did the dairy. My friend's husband, his parents kept the dairy in St Mary's Road, next door to where the sorting office is; he used to do one delivery and his mother used to come round to North Hayling with a pony and trap. You took your jug out and she'd tip the milk in. Used to come round twice a day.

Mrs Joyce Poore (née Nichol), born 1919

Washing the Hard Way

When I got married we just had a little rubber wringer. And I haven't got a washing-machine now. Well, I've got a little geyser in the sink but that's no good for a washing-machine, it would cost goodness knows what, and then there isn't room. So we had to do it the hard way and boil our nappies. I don't mind rubbing out washing, I've got my spin-drier and the sheets are now poly-cotton, I don't find them hard to wash.

Mrs Eva Prior, born 1910

More Postmen

When I joined the postal service in 1967 there were eleven postmen, now there are about thirty-four.

Roy Chamberlain, born 1929

New to Hayling

When I first moved to Hayling, the coal was delivered – Hayling Coal and Transport. Old Billy the coal horse was still alive, he used to pull one of the carts with the coal on. The Hayling Billy train had stopped running, the Regal Cinema had just closed. The People's Dispensary for Sick Animals van used to come, I think it was twice a week, to treat the animals.

I used to go shopping once a week to Finefare in Havant, on the bus with my three children, a twin pushchair and a shopping trolley. I must have pushed one and pulled the other. It was cheaper in Havant, worth the bus fare, you know?

I used to find it quite interesting, going round Northney way. If you sat on the top you could see the pretty houses. I used to like looking in people's gardens.

Mrs Patricia Gordon, born 1943

As it Was

Sinah Warren was a lovely private house, the Arbuthnots'. Mr Arbuthnot was a real eccentric old gentleman. He had a pig farm down there and a chicken farm, we used to get our eggs. The two daughters, they used to be our Brown Owls of the Brownies. We used to go down there and it was beautiful. Of course, they've built over it now. There was a pond on the corner. They knocked down what used to be the gardener's cottage and built about ten houses.

Down Eastoke, I can remember when there was just Dr White and Tickner's Farm, the rest was fields.

Mrs Grace Townsend, born 1924

The Knitting Factory

The bungalow I sold to finance my company had the Baxter knitting factory behind it [now McVere Engineering]. Mr Petley, who ran it, was always inviting me in to look round (and also when he had little mechanical problems!) It frightened the life out of me when I went in there. He had turn of the century knitting-machines. There were arms and things flying all over the place; his oiling machines were driven by one giant electric motor, by shafts in the ceiling, all rocking about, with bicycle spare wheels on them, driving yards and yards of bicycle-chain! So from each machine ushered a bicycle-chain, stretching up to the heavens; one of the shafts makin' a terrific racket; horrendously noisy and oil flying about all over the place!

The girls all wore turbans. They wouldn't allow it now. They were all adept at staying in their places and walking where there was no oil spray and the whole building reeked and was solid with oil droplets. He had old cocoa tins, suspended on bits of wire, with pipes in the bottom, dripping oil along the moving chain all the while, to lubricate it. He used to scrounge it from local garages – old engine oil – and thin it down with paraffin.

They made – you wouldn't believe, out of this filthy, black hole, came the most beautiful knitwear. Most of it was exported to America. He's a lovely chap. He trained all the knitting factory girls to work at Skipper's.

F.T. Skipper, born 1932

Naval People

The road going down to the ferry was part of the golf course in the 1930s; the golfers used to play across. There were all sand dunes. It was the Navy flattened it. It's spoiled, I mean there was nothing round here, just a few houses down St Catherine's Avenue; and between it and Staunton Avenue, just fields, long grass and trees. My children used to get out there for the day.

One knew everyone on Hayling. Basically, it was naval people; most of the houses along St Catherine's were rented and it was just the holiday business really, ours was the biggest business on Hayling. It was mainly business, solicitors and doctors, a few local people. I mean, there were the boatyards and fishing. And there were hotels. The Navy used to rent. I think they had to be out for a couple of weeks each year when the owners used to come back.

Mrs Hazel Warner, born 1929

Milkman at Eastoke

Holiday places at Eastoke was proper carriages – there's one up there still – or old goods wagons. They built in windows in them. Put verandahs on them. There was a lot of them, specially down on the Seafront. Eastoke, Creek Road. There were lovely chalets on stilts opposite Miller's. People did live in them. A lot of people who, technically, had been chucked out of their houses, they took winter lets down there. I was a milkman up there in the 1960s and we never let a bottle of milk go unless we had the cash for it, before the roads were made up.

John Plimbley, 1927-1999

Lifeboat and Coastguards

The Suntrap nurses' home became a block of flats and looks as it was, opposite the old lifeboat station. The lifeboat used to go down to the sea from there. Those cottages that stand back opposite are called Coast Guard Cottages; that's where the coastguards used to live. I remember the new lifeboat coming, but I was too young to bother about that – you know what you are at sixteen? You couldn't care less, really, could you?

Mrs Joyce Poore (née Nichol), born 1919

Mrs Nipper in her Eastoke shop has seen many changes.

Safe at Night

There were no street lights in the war time, but you weren't afraid to walk up from off the bus at the Yew Tree, you thought nothing of it but you'd be scared to death now. I forgot to lock the church one night and went down about half past ten; my son nearly went mad!

Mrs Eva Prior, born 1910

Fun at Beachlands

On Beachlands, let's see, there were tea-rooms, ghost train, boats – you could row your little boat around in the big water. There was so much to do then. A fortune-teller too! I never did go to one. Pr'haps if there was anything I didn't want to hear, I didn't want to know! It really was good fun. The beach was packed solid, horses were backwards and forwards and a train as well. There was a Crescent Club, with the Black and White Minstrels and the Tiller Girls. They were on the telly the other morning – the Tiller Girls, they're as good as ever! And they're all in their sixties!

Mrs Lilian Townsend-Holmes, born 1930

A Rural Divide?

There was a divide between rural people, gipsies, of which we had quite a lot and retired services people, Navy and Army, so there were strata, you know. People were very conscious of this. I don't think it was ownership of big houses so much as what they actually were themselves, because church was very good, St Mary's – in those days, people went to church as a social place, didn't they? As much as for religion? I mean, Church of England, in rural places, that's where you went, to church. My granny was Baptist, and when she came over and found that I was going to the Church of England and there was a Baptist church here, she thought that I was the wickedest child you'd ever met. But the music was beautiful.

Mrs Brenda Wood, born 1915

Remembering the Sixties

People could stay over the weekend at the Crescent Club on Norfolk Crescent, it was the whole block. The bar was on the balcony and down the basement was the kitchens; this [ground-floor flat] was a big lounge bar, and the rest were bedrooms, for people to stay the night. Most of the Black and White Minstrels and Tiller girls used to stay over. It was exciting. And we had the clubs at the other end of the Island. The Beach Club [earlier the Nab Club, later Miller's] and next door was the Hayling Island Club – but I think that's called Dixie's now. It is open till 2.00 a.m., it's most likely for the young ones.

Night-clubs were better. We used to jitterbug and jive. Oh, I could still do a little turn now, if needs be. Humperdinck, Tom Jones and the Beach Boys – that was good music in the 1960s, beautiful time.

Mrs Lilian Townsend-Holmes, born 1930

Cars and Bikes at Northney

The outbreak of war, when I was working on the farm, as far as I can remember there was only two cars in the village, there might have been the odd parson car. The farmer had a lorry and a car, and the local butcher or the landlord, I don't know which one had the car, they used to go about together, 'cos they were related; and do a fair bit of drinking. I can remember them going into the ditch in the corner of Gutner Lane, when they were a little bit over the top!

You used to walk everywhere or cycle. The three local policemen had bicycles; a sergeant and two constables for the whole of Hayling! One of them used to come round and visit us, y'know, just to see everything was in order. The doctor used to come round on the trades bike, with his black bag in the basket.

Lawrence Shepherd, born 1927

Horse Ride to Northney

When we came to Hayling in 1971, we could ride across to Northney, go to a little shop there and ride back, without getting involved in heavy traffic. But the camp's gone, the shop's closed, and everybody has put up their boundaries. I regret not being able to ride more or less round the whole of the Island. On Sundays, it was nothing to see half a dozen kids on ponies, up on the gun-site, being able to get round. It's totally dangerous to use the road now.

We lived in an old bungalow, before the houses. There were just old shacks, which were through the present Queen's Way and to the north of New Cut – each just tracks, wide enough for a milk-float, with nothing to the south and the middle but a bit of field, about 11 acres with a few cows in. I used to graze my ponies in the present Queen's Way and it was nothing for the ponies to escape round here and nobody worried. My family drove cows down the road, to exchange bulling cows with farmer Alan North. Well, I mean, you can't imagine doing that through all these bloomin' gardens!

Jill Colliver, born 1939

All Change at Northney

Where the village hall is now, opposite that was a field and Mrs Nangel lived in the one big house that was there. We used her house as an ambulance station during the war. And the big house that's just been built next door is where I stayed with the ponies, when I worked on the farm. And on the other side, in line with the hall, there was only three flint cottages and next to that was the big thatched barn which Hedger had for the store of potatoes. And then the opposite side

again of the lane where the big one is, there's three big houses, which was the grounds of a little nursery. And behind that was all farmland. So I've seen it all changing.

Lawrence Shepherd, born 1927

The Kench and Campaigns

The Kench is beautiful, it's a wild sanctuary for birds; we had a big meeting about that, up in arms. They were going to build a marina and once they did that, the road would have to be widened, you'd get loads of extra people – we don't want people do we? You can't have birds! So that went by the board.

The bypass was going through at the back somewhere, leaving Stoke village, then near the old railway line. Of course when the traffic all met at the bridge they would have still had congestion.

Spinnaker Close, Northney, built on the site of a former holiday camp.

Fred Skipper's old barn, West Town, just prior to demolition.

They campaigned against the closure of the West Town post office in 1988. So that was stopped. As for the railway on the front, they were going to uproot the front. I don't think they should have built Eastoke side at all because of the flooding. Now they've really settled in on Ham Field. People don't have to live on Hayling, the schools were full and we wanted to keep our fields.

Mrs Joan Duckett, 1915-1999

Shops and Shacks

Since 1983, the leather and shoe repair shop at Stoke has disappeared. And there were a lot of old shacks where houses now are in the Avenue Road area. If you lived there long enough, like squatters, it was yours.

E. Marsden, born 1917

The Old Barn

There used to be a thatched barn at the entrance to Skipper's. I offered it for a museum but the local authority insisted it must be removed. I think it was where every woodworm on Hayling was born. My yard was originally Camp's coal yard and builders' merchants.

F.T. Skipper, born 1932

The Great Infill

There has been too much new building on Hayling: the great infill. My husband remembers when Southwood Road was a cart track, and of course, Shanty Town, where the railway carriages, which were used as holiday homes, were. I think one or two are still there; they've been enclosed.

I'm told that families would come for all of the summer. One family stayed with a local shopkeeper each summer and set themselves up with bathing gear. These kind of families don't seem to be there any more. Where the houses are now, at Sandy Point Estate, there were cornfields; I remember seeing a kingfisher on the little bridge, before you turn round where the lifeboat station is. The countrified villages are running into one another and atmosphere is going.

My daughter climbed into trees at Mengham Lane, now houses and bungalows, part of the Regal Cinema site; there were fields where Cherrywood Gardens is. There were three bungalows built in one garden; one very lovely house has been pulled down and a block of flats was built there. We used to learn Scottish dancing in the garden. Hayling was much more rural. When we see Ham Field disappear, I think that is very sad.

But quite a lot is done for the elderly; there's still a great deal of care and concern. The Health Centre is good.

Mrs A., born 1920

Relocating to Hayling

The main reason I came to Hayling is that my wife relocated because she took a promotion, and subsequently had another promotion and clearly I needed to relocate myself. It wasn't easy. It took me approximately three years because I work in a specialized field

When it was known that she was going to Hayling, one of my wife's pupils said, 'You're not going to live on Ham Field are you? My mother's campaigning against those houses being built'.

It was a problem. I can understand why, with hindsight; I mean, I just happened to be driving around, saw the site and liked the area. And I would have possibly lived on Hayling even if these hadn't been here. But I can understand why people who live in a rural environment don't want to see houses springing up like mushrooms.

Terence Giltinan, born 1946

Ideal Home

My wife and I lived in Hayling holiday lets, after selling a house and losing the one we intended to buy, ten years before we came to the Island permanently in 1996. Hayling seemed the place that we were waiting for.

J.E. Baxter, born 1927

Nice Place to Live

Dad moved into Hayling because the family bought some flats on the Seafront, for investment, and my grandmother lived in Winchester. They thought Hayling was a nice place to live.

Mr H., born 1975

Lovely Island

My husband has his own business. We started a family and Hayling was our ideal for bringing up children. Lovely island. I came to Hayling via Wales, London and Portsmouth.

Mrs J. Fellows

Clean Air

I was born in Buckinghamshire, lived in Hendon until 1986. I was in the RAF, then civil flying, then teaching. My wife's a teacher too. We retired to the Island, swim daily; we love the clean air and politeness of people in shops. Heavy traffic at summer weekends is a snag but people who grumble about Hayling roads have never lived in London!

L.C. Hill

School Move

We came to North Hayling in 1971 from Sussex, to be near Glenhurst School, Havant, where my children went. It was a 3d bus fare to Havant, buses every quarter of an hour, so there was no problem and at that stage, you could let children go on their own. I mean, mine at five years old crossed this main Havant Road. It was a generation ago.

We came to Queen's Road before Avenue Road and the roads off it were built.

The shacks were possibly built for safety, during the war. In the 1950s and '60s, this area was Shanty Town. As were several areas on the Island. One near my house, which belonged to an old Pole who came over during the war. He's long since died; we used to call him Vladivostock – a very pleasant fellow. The original people have long since either died or gone.

Jill Colliver, born 1939

Sailor's Wife

I was born in Newcastle, spent most of my schooldays in Nottingham and was married to a sailor. He obviously wanted me to be near him – he was based in Portsmouth.

I moved to Southsea then in 1964 to Hayling. There were a lot of Air Force people in the same little estate, Warren Sands, where we had a flat. We didn't have a car.

Mrs Patricia Gordon, born 1943

A Building Boom

I like Hayling. Mind, it's spoiled. There's been too much building. The war was just finished, you know, with Japan and all that, 1946, no '47, I came back home and then demobbed. I went on building.

In my time we built Elm Close Estate, there was Cherry Wood Estate, Dancer's Way down West Town – we built a lot. We were some of the culprits, takin' away the green fields! The beach – it's an annual affair, to bring stones in.

Robert Dance, born 1920

Charlie Barley at the Barley Mow

In West Town we had Manor and Ham Farm, on the corner where the Barley Mow is now. Then they pulled it all down, o'course; they built all those houses on it now. It was just for cows only, years ago, and we had our own little market-place where they used to do all their own lovely milk and cream and that. So the other Barley Mow was round the corner [now Jasper's]. Charlie Barley and his wife had it. We called him Charlie Barley.

Mrs Lilian Townsend-Holmes, born 1930

North Hayling Congregational church at Stoke, disbanded some years ago.

Rough Roads

Bacon Lane was rough in the 1930s, Stamford Avenue made up, and Staunton Avenue unmade. Shingle – big potholes and everything. The gates of the McEuen estate, with the big balls on top, are still there.

Peter Tibble, born 1932

Grow Your Own

Of course in 1939 you went everywhere by bike. There were no shops, never have been, in North Hayling; well, one tiny sort of sweet-shop. You grew your own vegetables, had your own chickens and gave up your egg ration for meal, but apart from that, the butcher came round three times a week from Stoke – Drewery's; Smith and Vosper's the bakers

called twice a week with a motor van for bread, cakes and tinned food. The fishman came by bike from Emsworth every Friday.

Mrs Joyce Poore (née Nichol), born 1919

Affordable Housing

I came to Hayling for a two-day course with the Royal Navy during World War Two; I moved here in 1962 because it had a house I could afford.

Mr B.

Escape from Dundee

In the 1960s I wanted to move from Timex, and Dundee with its cold, damp climate. My son had asthma and they said Hayling had a school for children with chest problems. We settled on the Island and our son's health improved, so he had normal schooling. Dorothy and I have retired here.

Owen Williams

Clear View to West Town

In the 1960s the wooden buildings at the Sunshine Holiday Camp were disappearing and brick ones were being built. A remaining wooden building on site is used as a first-aid hut. Even in Seagrove Avenue, I remember a wooden place that they built a brick skin all round.

When I arrived on the Island, from Palmerston Road you could see almost over to West Town; St Mary's Road, all those houses, Cherrywood Gardens, the Hayling

Billy pub – there was nothing there. The shops next to Pullinger's was one drapers. Now it's four shops.

Ernie Turner, born 1943

Skylark at Ham Field

We've found a spot alongside the golf course which is ideal for our two dogs to run. I heard the skylark this morning, which I enjoyed, and shortly there'll be all sorts of wild flowers. And going back across the bridge, particularly if the sun's shining, you get the reflections.

When we've been to the local shops, everybody's very friendly, particularly the post office. Shopping, we do prefer just going to Mengham. The Hardware shop – I spend a lot of my time there. Where possible we use the shops on the Island. The other thing I like is that I play golf on the par three course.

Mr D., born 1938

Love it or Hate it

Hayling, you either love or you hate it. There's no happy medium. I've always loved Hayling. It's overbuilt, like most places it just doesn't seem the same, but whether that is slightly through rose-tinted glasses? You don't know.

Mrs Patricia Gordon, born 1943

Acknowledgements

My grateful thanks to all those listed below who have shared their views and memories with me, loaned photographs, made me welcome in their homes, told me of people who had stories to tell, or helped in any way. My thanks also to those who were happy to talk to me but did not wish to be named, and who are referred to in this book by initials which are not theirs to preserve their anonymity.

Especial thanks to David Edwards for the use of his postcards, and to Capt. Derek Oakley, MBE, RM. For photographs and other illustrations, I am endebted to Hayling Island Library, and to several local organizations that have contributed to this book: Hayling Island's Amateur Dramatic Society, Community Centre, Horticultural Society, Sailing Club, Scouts, and Women's Institute; my thanks also to the Isle of Wight Railway Company Ltd for allowing me to use their photograph of the Hayling Billy engine. The following people kindly loaned me photographs, many of which appear in this book: R.A. Adams; J.E. Baxter; A.A.F. Bell; Mrs Janet Bocking; Michael Camp; Mrs Mavis Chamberlain; Mrs Audrey Cozens; Mrs Joan Duckett; David Edwards; Clive Fowler; Terence Giltinan; Mrs Patricia Gordon; Capt. Derek Oakley MBE, RM; John Plimbley; Mrs Joyce Poore; Noel Pycroft; Arnold Sharples; Lawrence Shepherd; Brian Shorthouse; Joyce and Sam Simms; F.T. Skipper; Neil Sparshatt; Mrs Joan Stokeley; Mrs Grace Townsend; Ernie Turner; C. Vaughan; Mrs Mary Voller; D. White; Mrs Brenda Wood.

The story of *Hayling Island Voices* is told through the reminiscences of Hayling Islanders past and present. The following abbreviations indicate my method of collecting material: (R) recording, (N) notes, (L) by letter. My thanks to all those who contributed to this project, many of whose memories feature in this book: R.A. Adams and son (R); J.W. Allen (N); Mrs M. Baird (N); Clive Barrett, (N); J.E. Baxter (R); A.A.F. Bell (R); Mrs Janet Bocking (R); Mrs Beryl Bonniface (R); Michael Camp (R); Mr and Mrs Roy Chamberlain (R); E. Chapman (N); Rosemary Clubb, (R); D. Collins (N); Mrs Jill Colliver (R); Col. John d'E Coke RM (R); Mrs Jean Copsey; Mrs Audrey Cozens, (née Tyrrell) (R); Robert Dance (R); Eric Dossetter (R); Mrs Joan Duckett, (R); John Derben, OBE (R); Mrs J. Fellows (N); Nigel Ford; Mrs Queenie Gates (R); Terence Giltinan (R); Mrs Patricia Gordon (R); James Gorman (R); Ian Griffiths (R); L.C. Hill (N); Mr and Mrs E.J. Hitchcock (R); Elyane Jones (R); Martin Loft (L); Beryl, Lady Mackworth (R); Mrs E. Marsden (N); Mrs Pam Marsden (N); Mrs Joan McAndrew (N); Mrs Dorothy S. Millns (N); T. Monro (N); Mrs J. Nipper (N); Mr and Mrs John Plimbley (R); Mrs Joyce Poore (R); Mr and Mrs Poulton (N); Mrs Eva Prior (R); Noel Pycroft (R); David Roberts (R); Arnold Sharples (L); Lawrence Shepherd (R); Mrs M. Short (N); Brian Shorthouse (L); Jack Sinclair (L); Roy Skennerton (N); F.T. Skipper (R); Roy Smith (R); Peter Tibble (R); Mrs Grace Townsend (R); Mrs D.L. Townsend-Holmes (R); Ernie Turner (R); Miss Caroline Turrell (N); Colin Vaughn (R); Mrs Mary Voller (L); Mrs V. Walter (L); Mrs Hazel Warner (R); Mrs Dot Watson (R); Owen Williams (N); Mrs Brenda Wood (R); Plus Mrs A. (R); Mr and Mrs D. (R); Mr J. (N); Mr H. (N); Mr B. (N).

My apologies to anyone I have inadvertently forgotten to include in these Acknowledgements.